OUR HUMAN VALUES

Volume 2

WHO AM I?
HOW DID I CHOOSE MY IDENTITY?

Dr. Bob O'Connor

Total Health Publications

Copyright 2021

TABLE OF CONTENTS

A PREFACE—WHERE AND WHY THIS VOLUME?

If you have stayed with me through Volume I, you are probably aware of how important it is to look to the foundations of our beliefs in order to understand WHY we believe WHAT we believe--and WHY we behave as we DO. Philosophers of ethics would like to tell us HOW to behave. Our emphasis has been directed primarily on why we may behave as we do. As we look at how we might construct our identities, some of us may become more introspective in terms of living effectively, more socially concerned, more invigorated to live a thoughtfully dynamic lifeVarying researchers have defined "self- concept" and "identity" as the same, or with slight differences. We will view them as identical. But there is another concern with identity! Do you like yourself--your identity? This is called "self-esteem" and is a major concern in mental health. If you have a clear sense of who you are, and you approve of yourself, major and minor negatives can be weathered and you won't need alcohol, cannabis, heroin, or a gun in your mouth to forget or eliminate your problems. In Volume One we emphasized the importance of having been loved and therefore, being able to love. If you have been so blessed, your identity has a strong foundation. But foundations sometime crack, as the Surfside condo recently did in Miami. But there are sometimes those without the foundation of love who develop strong, even loving, identities. Nelson Mandela comes to mind. Intelligently developing one's identity--utilizing the evidence of psychology, history, and philosophy--can bring a life satisfaction and self-esteem to anyone with a deep commitment to achieving it.

In this volume, we intend to both challenge and broaden why we hold our values. Some of our most strongly held values are often only opinions, with only bits of carefully selected evidence to back them up. In this volume we plan to shake up some beliefs, dig deeper into attitudes, and look at the broader blanket on which they lay. While we may sometimes wander afield, it is with purpose. For example, if you believe yourself to include in your identity a strong national purpose, re-examining the effect of an out-of-control national debt may stimulate your concern--this may then change your values, and possibly stimulate your behavior to change America's national credit card mythology.

We all have identities, some very strong, and some relatively weak. For example:

➢   I am a Texan and a strong evangelical Baptist. I am a proud member of my union, USW. I live and die by the success of my high school football team, the Odessa Bronchos.

➢   I am a conservative pro-Trump Republican, I absolutely refuse to take a Covid-19 vaccination. I am free--and will protect my freedom with any means at my disposal.

➢   I graduated from the University of Notre Dame. I am a very strong Catholic and would never use contraceptives or have an abortion. I love my work with Microsoft.

➢   I'm from California, but haven't been back there for ten years. I just follow the big waves in Hawaii, Australia, Portugal, or wherever I can find them. I'm a big kahuna around the "Pipeline."

➢I am so blessed that I was loved and nurtured by my parents, that is why I am so content with my nursing career.

➢I'm a Blood. My dad was a Blood. We are the best and toughest gang in LA. I have killed three Crips and somebody else, but the police never pinned them on me. My only prison time was for selling crack. I'm tough and smart.

Prejudicial identities may mark us--sometimes helping, sometimes hurting. Germans work hard. Haitians are lazy. Chinese are smart. Irish are friendly--or drunk!

While skiing in France some years ago I saw a T-shirt on a girl that illustrated some possible ethnic prejudices--or identities. On the front of the shirt it said:

Heaven is:
Where the skiing is French,
The policemen are British,
The mechanics are German,
The lovers are Italian--
---And, it's all organized by the Swiss.

On the back of the shirt was written:
Hell is:
Where the skiing is British,
The policemen are German,
The mechanics are French,
The lovers are Swiss.
--And it's all organized by the Italians.

Our identities may help or harm us in life. The self-styled macho tough guy may find it difficult to keep a relationship with an intelligent woman, and may find himself in jail because of abusive behavior.

Identities that are national can have strong historical effects. The Islamic identity if Afghanistan was extremely important in fighting off both the Russians and the Americans during the last 50 years. As Rome matured and the Roman military was composed of mercenaries, the Roman identity that built the nation decayed and the nation died. The Crusaders, fired by their Christian identity, fought the Muslims for 300 years, and the passion of the Islamic identities held the Holy Land. National, religious, educational, and geographical identities are only a part of what we are and how we will act.

The recent pro-Trump identity has played havoc in America, giving many an identity that often overflowed the cup of conscience. But it cloaked many in a shroud of self-esteem. So, we will soon look a bit deeper into the demands and demeanor of "the Donald" to glimpse how identities may be constructed, psychologically and logically. We may then better understand how our values can be formed, shaped and manipulated to achieve our own ends or the others who may be pulling our strings. A recent Pew poll strongly indicated that many anti-Trump voters wouldn't even consider dating a pro-Trump person. This was especially true of women.

It isn't Trump *per se,* but what he has come to represent--reactionary ideas, anti-minority, anti-abortion, anti-equalitarianism, and other ideas that the equalitarian liberals find essential. And, we find more equalitarian thinking among the educated adults.

Many Republicans followed Trump's call for freedom and refused vaccinations. In July of 2021, four states with Republican governors, and one with a Democratic governor, led the nation with over 1600 new Covid cases per day. One might wonder if the Trump-Republican anti-vaccination, anti-mask, anti-social distancing ideas killed off some of its base members and might have turned others against the party after they followed the flag, but then caught the bug.

SECTION I   DEVELOPING OUR IDENTITIES

Our identities, as our values, begin with our genetics and epigenetics, then form as our intrauterine, then post-birth environments form and re-form us.

As mentioned several times previously, our genes, and the epigenetic changes that change how and whether they operate, decimate the theory of John Locke's *tabula rasa* theory. But the specter of that theory has survived through Freud, through the many concepts of psychological therapies, and is thoroughly understood by the parenting populace. The problem is that while psychological researchers generally recognize the importance of "nature" and often give it a 50% chance of determining our behaviors and our lives, we find it difficult, or impossible, to comprehend fully! So we generally concentrate on nurture. Are we missing half of the book of life?

CHAPTER 1 NATURE AND NURTURE

As discussed in Volume One, we are born with genetic and epigenetic propensities. They may be toward: violence, loving altruism, the ability to learn (IQ), mental or physical illnesses, drug use, or any number of such tendencies. Some of us are afflicted with injuries at birth, such as cerebral palsies that can affect our physical and mental abilities.

NATURE

Our DNA can give us specific traits, like eye color and ear shape. It may give us potentials, like how tall or smart we might be. But our environment can limit or enhance those potentials. Proper nutrition, exercise and sunlight may enhance our growth potentials. Effective educations at school and home can enhance our academic acumen. But there may be other genetic factors, such as the need to protect one's property, the need to protect one's children, toward the use of physical power--instincts that are probably genetic, but are denied by many. After all, if we are made in the Image of God, how could we have instincts. It will probably take many years before scientists can separate genetic from epigenetic tendencies and behaviors. Stay tuned!

We probably shouldn't leave this DNA mention without taking a casual look at our distant ancestors. As you know, Lewis Leakey spent his life searching for our earliest ancestors.

Hans Reck, a German, discovered a somewhat modern skeleton in Olduvai Gorge in 1913. It was dated as from a half-million years ago. In 1948 the Leakey's discovered an 18 million year-old fossil called Proconsul. Tt was a small ape. Then in 1959, Mary Leakey discovered a skull that was 1,750,000 years old. Then in 1960, Jonathan Leakey, the 19-year-old son of Mary and Louis discovered and even more human skull. It had a brain size of 675 cm³. At that time 700 cubic centimeters was considered the standard for a skull to be considered at humanoid (genus *Homo*). A number of fossils have been discovered that had anthropologists argue whether they were apes or men.

Of course, brain size isn't everything. The Neanderthals had brain sizes averaging 1450 cubic centimeters, with a high, so far found, of a 1,750 cubic centimeter fella. Homo sapiens average about 1,330 cubic centimeters. But if brain size were everything, elephants with 5,000 cubic centimeter brains would be the smartest of us all. But they do say that an elephant never forgets. Maybe that's because he has such a big trunk in which to store his memories!

But we have a few other people in our past. There were offshoots of the ape-men and man-apes that the Leakeys and others found. We have found *homo sapiens* bones throughout Europe and Asia. Some of those go back over 200,000 years. East Asian finds are about as old. Our ancestry is not a simple straight line from Australopithecus to Neanderthals to us (*homo sapiens*). Just as there are many species of monkeys, there are many species of "*homos.*" While the evidence now strongly indicates that our branch started in Africa, who knows for sure? The Neanderthals that lived throughout Europe and Asia, did not seem to have originated there. While Europeans and East Asians average about 2% Neanderthal DNA (ranging from 1 to 4%), Africans are now found to have about 0.3%. It appears that after developing elsewhere, some went south the mingle. Until recently, we didn't believe that Africans had any Neanderthal DNA. Both *homo neaderthalensis* and *homo sapiens* interbred with others from the genus *homo* during the 400,000 or so years that they roamed the Eastern Hemisphere. The thinking is that they may have bred themselves into extinction--melding into the other species they found. Lots of breeding can be done in a few hundred thousand years!

Today only about 7% of our *homo sapiens* DNA is specifically *homo sapiens.* So, if sometimes you feel like a tiger, and other times make an ass of yourself, the cause is undoubtedly somewhere in that other 93%.

Usually our family and the environment in which we were raised are critical to our identities. If we escape through friends, schooling or employment, it may move us up or down the social class ladder and change our identities.

NURTURE

Your physical, emotional, economic, academic, and social environment can increase your genetic potentials. Of course, they can also handicap them. Let's take a hypothetical example. Assume that we have several absolutely identical, genetically and epigenetically, babies. I guess they would have to be clones!

1. Raised by a single concerned mother in a government subsidized project in a New Your ghetto,

2. Raised by a single drug addicted mother in a government subsidized project in a New Your ghetto,

3. Raised by a European nanny, because the parents were often absent because of their high-level government jobs. But from age 6, attended the finest private boarding schools,

4. Raised by two teachers, an elementary school and a high school educators. For its first five years it was attended to by its maternal grandmother until 4 PM when its parents returned from work. They were together every weekend,

5. Spent the first year with one, then the other, parent--who were paid by the government to bond with the child, then at age one was in kindergarten from 8 to 4 until the parents finished work (a childhood common in many European countries),

6. Raised by one stay-at-home parent in a small midwestern farm town.

Do you think that these six children, who started genetically equal will have equal identities at 10, 18, or 35?

Do nature and nurture count equally? Is it 50-50? We can never know for certain. In on person the genetic make up may overwhelm the environment. Edison, Napoleon, Helen Keller, Lincoln and Henry Ford might be examples. In other cases, the environment might be controlling. John Kennedy, George W. Bush, Billy Jean King, Basher al-Assad, and Barack Obama might be examples.

Societies, like most people, try to fix the problem after it happens, rather than trying to prevent them. Fixing a Hitler, an Assad, or a Manson is many years too late,

YOUR IDENTITY, LIKE YOUR MIND, HAS CONSCIOUS AND UNCONSCIOUS ASPECTS

You know, or assume, your place in your family and in your job. Maybe your identity over- or under-estimates your likeability or your attractiveness. Maybe your religiosity is important. Maybe you have heard of your country's national debt, but you think that it is somebody else's problem. Perhaps your group identity seeks equality of your religious, ethnic, or economic views, but you learned in school that the country was founded on the principle of liberty, and you know that liberty and equality are often antithetical ideals. Maybe you want to drive on better roads and over sounder bridges, but you don't want to pay higher gas taxes.

We may have heard of the dire projection of not paying enough taxes or not having a standing army, or adequate pensions--but it's not my worry!

But there are consequences to all of our actions or inactions. Is it possible that your drug-addicted son did not have the self-esteem he could have developed if you hadn't spent so much time at the office, in a bar, or playing video games? It is possible the you had won, if you had only bet on a different horse? Is it possible that you wouldn't be sitting in prison if you had only studied in high school and gone to college?

We have our identities. Did we arrive at them by accident or by thinking trough them?

Let's take a couple of hypothetical examples.

Let's assume that we look at four black boys. Two are born in the ghetto of South-Central Los Angeles. They do not know who their fathers are. They are perfectly content playing with their friends on the street or on the playground. By the time one is about 12 years old he has seen nothing beyond his local environment. He may decide that his greatest goal is to become a member of the local Crips gang. He has seen a number of shooting and knifing deaths in his neighborhood.

His neighbor, also 12, has watched more television and has seen black men as detectives, doctors or lawyers. He thinks that this might be a better life than the one he is living. His mother tells him that he can fulfill his dreams by studying hard at school and going to college. He does. He is now an assistant district attorney. He had to recuse himself from prosecuting his boyhood friend on murder charges in a drug related crime.

At the other end of the country, another black boy, this one the son of the Fortune 500 CEO, lives in Martha's Vineyard, Massachusetts, and all of his friends are similarly rich. He is expected to go to an Ivy League school and follow his daddy's footsteps, so he majors in economics at Yale. His best friend, also black, is his college roommate. Both go into Wall Street banking. Both know that the size of one's wallet equals the size of one's worth. Both are highly successful.

One decides to make more money by starting a hedge fund, then by publicizing it by using Ponzi schemes. He makes billions of dollars, but many of his investors find out how he made his money. He follows Bernie Maddock's path and ends in prison, where he dies.

His friend stayed with Goldman Sachs. He retired with a million dollar a year pension. He is now on his yacht anchored in the Monaco harbor.

These hypothetical illustrations show how one's initial environment might influence one's values. Decisions made along life's pathways can move us into earthly heavens or hells. Starting life closer to heaven does not guarantee an angelic future. Our values become more obvious as we grow and mature. Are they intelligently chosen or merely acquired? Do they beckon us up the mountain, requiring us to fight for every step? Or do they sanctify our satisfaction with video games and television sports?

Are some of our values strong enough to make us overcome genetic inadequacies or environmental handicaps? When we look back at our life choices and accomplishments from the rocking chair of our retirements will we smile, enjoying whom we have become? Or will we choose to end our lives--deciding that they have no value?

Will we even make it to old age? Ernest Hemingway shot himself at 61, Virginia Woolf battled mental problems and drowned herself at 59. Vincent Van Gogh battled many mental illness problems before shooting himself at 37. Marilyn Monroe at 36 and Freddie Prinz at 22 used drugs to end it all. Neither beauty, money nor fame are enough to prevent the end of one's identity--one's life. Rich people kill themselves. Beautiful people kill themselves. Famous people kill themselves. Some have been haunted by the specter of mental illness. Did they value their lives enough to seek help? Many have found that their lives are not what they might be. Did they seek help? Did they know where they wanted to go with their lives? Had they thought about how they wanted to live? Had they thought about how they might accomplish it? Had they worked to achieve it? With nearly 50,000 Americans killing themselves annually, how many pulled the trigger or downed the pill, because they did not have worthwhile values to pursue? How many teenagers believed their cyberbullies' taunts that they were valueless. And how many of the bullies feel value only when their power drives are satisfied by picking on a weaker ego?

CHAPTER 2   WE ALL HAVE IDENTITIES--WHAT IS THEIR VALUE?

Our identities might cover our cowardice or stupidity, but hopefully, they project a socially significant purpose. When Freud and Montagu tell us that mental health results when we can love unselfishly and have a work ethic--do we believe them? Do we agree?

We all have opinions or desires-- some strong, some relatively weak. Have we thought them through?

For example:

➢ Black Lives Matter, in fact all lives matter! What about Hitler's? Did his life matter? If so, did it matter more than the 11 million who died in the war because of him?

➢ I want to smoke marijuana. I also want children. Will the epigenetic changes in my sperm negatively affect my child? Cannabis smoking fathers increase their chances of methylating the DLGAP2 gene which is linked to autism. It can be transmitted in the sperm. According to a recent Canadian study, marijuana smoking mothers have a 50% increased chance of having an autistic child. So they blame it on vaccinations! What about my increased chances of dying in an auto accident that I caused—or another cannabis user caused?

➢ I have the right to carry a gun—we all do. But, what if my child was accidentally shot in a drive-by shooting?

As mentioned in Volume I, some social media sites have warned people, falsely, that vaccinations are dangerous. A few women with autistic children have blamed vaccinations as the cause. The expected rate of autism is 1 to 2 per thousand births, and for the whole autism spectrum 6 per thousand. (The autism spectrum includes a number of communication and behavioral symptoms.)

Vaccinations have been highly effective in eliminating or reducing a number childhood diseases, many of which were often fatal. Among them were: polio, pertussis (whooping cough), smallpox, tetanus, diphtheria, influenza, and measles. More than a billion children have been vaccinated during the last decade.

Before we venture into Volume 3, we must look at the sources and quality of evidence we use. We must be aware of the numerous, and common, illogical ways that people use to convince us of something--and they sound so convincing! If somebody writes it on Twitter, it must be true! But what is the source of the evidence? How verifiable is it? Do I believe it only because it confirms my identity?

Will four years of diligent college study change my identity? Will it harden my feelings of negative racial prejudices against me? Will it stimulate me to be the best there is in my field so that there can be no rational prejudices against me because of my ethnicity or religion.

If we value intelligence, we must understand who we are, where we want to go, and what is the best way to get there. Dreams have their place in setting our goals, but they are useless in determining how to best get there. We must act on the best evidence available.

When President Trump said that he was cheated out of the election, he had no evidence. When he, his son, and his attorney told people to march on the Capitol, people looking for meaning and value in their fragile identities invaded the Capitol. QAnon, with its evidence-absent posts, spurred them on. The result: several deaths; multiple injuries; increased income for lawyers; prison sentences and job losses; federal expenses for more chain-link barriers, more police, legal actions and extensive repairs; more than 400 have, so far, been charged--with possible federal sentences of up to ten years. What values did these people think through thoroughly? Or, were they merely, lemming-like, following the exhortations of power-hungry people of questionable intelligence and self-centered values?

FATHOMING OUR FAITH AND FACTS--OUR IDENTITIES AND BELIEFS

We must be aware that when we use a word, the person with whom we are communicating will seldom understand it in the exact way that we do. So we have a semantic problem. Terms like: socialism, God, socialized medicine, love, freedom, democracy or equality will NEVER be understood in the exact same way that the speaker means. Other terms like: inch, kilogram, sound barrier, or longitude have precise meanings. So those of us in a discussion must understand the meaning of the words we use.

Next, we must be able to evaluate the evidence being used to bolster an argument. Is it empirically verifiable through research and knowledgeable evaluation? Is it only based on historical evidence? Is it a "rational" concept that sprung from the mind of a philosopher in a faraway ivory tower? Is it an outright lie, as we find in many social media sites-- or that are often proclaimed by partisan commentators? Is it only false rationalizations that immature egos use to excuse themselves from blame?

Recent PEW surveys (2016 and 2019) found that: about 33% of Americans trust government officials, about 50% trust business or religious leaders or news outlets, 82% trust the military, and 86% trust scientists. And, the greater their scientific knowledge, the more they trust science. To what degree should our own values be based on the probabilities of science and to what degree should they be based on tradition and myths? And, what about our society? Should we follow the demagogue with the loudest voice or the greatest presence on social media or should we use the scientific method and the tools of logic to direct our thinking--our choosing of our values, and our behavior?

SECTION II. UNDERSTANDING IDENTITIES

How we see ourselves, whether realistically or through the prism of a mental illness, determines how we act and how others evaluate us. We must feel that we are important. What makes you feel important?

- ➢ I have 12 children.
- ➢ I am a doctor.
- ➢ I drive a Tesla.
- ➢ My son is the quarterback.
- ➢ I'm a strong evangelical "born again" Christian.
- ➢ I voted for the winner.
- ➢ I was elected president of my country—and I plan to stay in charge indefinitely.
- ➢ I am Julius Caesar.
- ➢ I am a Republican

Often, we have negative identities.

- ➢ I am homeless.
- ➢ I am jobless.
- ➢ I am the dumbest kid in class.
- ➢ I am always depressed
- ➢ My mother is always stoned.
- ➢ My mother said that I caused the divorce

We may adopt our identities based on our accomplishments, our associations with others, like political parties or societal traditions, or as adjustments to our inferiority feelings. As we have recently seen in democratic elections, the promises of populists propel them to presidencies. Donald Trump promised to "make America great again." Boris Johnson told us that, "the United Kingdom is a sovereign nation, we must make Brexit happen." Chavez and Maduro on the left, or Trump and Johnson on the right, recognize that "our identities" are being held down by those above us—the Congress, the EU, the moneyed oligarchs.

And the result for the U.S.? Under Trump, America increased its national debt by $7 trillion dollars, but its economic growth and unemployment rates continued on the exact track that they had enjoyed for the previous six years. The U.S., with its "America first" policy, lost international standing and respect, and resulted in an "America alone" reality.

The result of voting for people who promise to indulge our identities, often has the opposite effect on our hopes. If we want to make the world better, it may indeed require castrating the control of moneyed oligarchs and prodding the parliaments to recognize the realities—

> ➤ There are too many people on the planet,
> ➤ They are creating climate changes that multiplies human suffering,
> ➤ Our education systems are far from effective or all encompassing,
> ➤ We produce children faster than we can produce the wealth and educators to educate them,
> ➤ There are too many unloved children, which hurts them and their society.

For the survival of the species, our identities must be positive, intelligent, and earned. Similarly, our politics and our governments must grow beyond pragmatically solving the problems of the present and look to the future to anticipate and prevent the problems that our current trajectory portends.

And it starts with our identities—as citizens of the world or of our nations—and as individuals.

To repeat the Preface of Volume I:

While philosophers of ethics desire that we think through our values from metaphysical bases, psychologists look for conscious and unconscious motivations, and the influences of our social systems on us. Both are needed to understand why we do what we do. But if we are to understand and think clearly about most of these issues, we must be multi-disciplinary. Economics, sociology, religion—even physiology must be considered. Since the values considered may range from what and how much to eat, to actions for climate change, to whom will get my vote, to whether to have children—to make intelligent value decisions, we need lots of verifiable evidence, and we must know which basic assumptions apply in our quest for a well-thought-out life—a fulfilling, productive, and enjoyable life.

CHAPTER 3   IF WE DON'T KNOW EVERYTHING--WE DON'T KNOW ANYTHING!

I will look at two murder cases from recent news stories--the conviction of police officer Derek Chauvin for the murder of George Floyd and the confession of a Los Angeles woman for drowning her three small children.

The law in the Chauvin case was only concerned with the last nine minutes of Floyd's life with Chauvin's knee on his neck, suffocating him. Why did Chauvin do it? Were there genetic or epigenetic factors from his ancestors that made him violent? We can't possibly know this. We could know if he had certain epigenetic anomalies today. But these were never tested. If they had been, there is no way to know if they were transmitted at conception, developed in the uterus, in his early life, or on the job. But presently, none of these would be accepted by the court as a mitigating circumstance. He did kill him, but unintentionally, so he was guilty of second-degree murder.

It is highly likely that Chauvin had a negative prejudice against young Black men accused of crimes. Minneapolis had been called Murderapolis in 1995 because of the number of murders in the city. In 2020, the year of the Floyd killing, the rate of murders was the second highest on record. The rate of violent crimes increased 60% from the time of Floyd's death. One hundred people were shot in Minneapolis during the first three weeks after George Floyd's death.

What about George Floyd? Did he have any epigenetic factors that made him prone to drug use or violence? Again, we have no specific evidence for Floyd, although there is ample evidence that both are possible, even probable, if one of his parents was abused or used drugs. Did his background of being raised by a single mother in a poor area of Houston have a negative effect on him? Probably.

 If he had gone quietly into the police car, he would still be alive today. Why didn't he? Was he afraid of more jail or prison time? Certainly his five-year prison sentence for aggravated armed robbery was not a pleasant experience for him. And his jail sentences in Texas for theft, for possession and passing small amounts of cocaine, and for failure to identify himself to a police officer--were not pleasant times.

Was he afraid of Federal prison for passing the counterfeit bill or for the possession of fentanyl? Was he aware that Federal sentencing laws could take into account some of his previous convictions? Was he afraid of being convicted in Minnesota for passing the counterfeit bill (under U.S. Code 18, para 372 or Minnesota 609.632 subj. 3). But the $20 bill he passed and those hidden in his car were relatively insignificant, so jail time was probably unlikely.

We can never know all the facts, but according to Minnesota law, only those last nine minutes were considered. What are the results? Floyd is dead. Chauvin is in prison. Murder rates and other violent crime is up in Minneapolis. Many police officers in Minneapolis, and around the country, have quit. Recruitment of officers is more difficult today.

Are the police negatively prejudiced? Do young Blacks actually commit more violent crime? With the ethnic percent of the population being: 61% White non-Hispanic, 18% Latino, and 13.4% Black--of the 895 police shootings in 2020: 51% were Whites, 27% were Blacks and 19% were Latino. This gives rates, according to their percentage of the population of: about 84% for whites, 200% for Blacks, while Latinos are just a shade over 100%. Here is an updated graph of police killings from 2017 to July 2021.

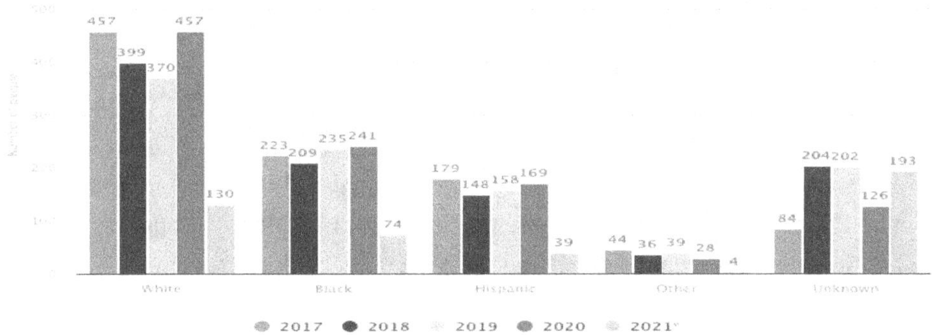

As noted in Volume One, there are more Whites shot and more Whites in prison, but the percentages of Blacks in each case are two to three times higher. Do Blacks commit more crime? The answer seems to be "yes" for violent crime, "no" for "white collar" crime. Obviously, all crime is bad. But is kidnapping a person and forcing them into white slavery worse than selling someone meth? What about kidnapping 25 women and forcing them into prostitution--is it worse than murdering a violent gang member?

In the Los Angeles case mentioned earlier, the murder was admitted. But other factors probably played into her decision. She said she drowned her children to protect them from their father. He said she had severe mental problems. He said she had increasingly bizarre claims: that she was "solely responsible" for the COVID-19 pandemic and that his hometown of Porterville was beset by a pedophile ring. She was influenced by QAnon. In escaping the police, she crashed her own car, then stole another. How much did her mental illness, actual evidence of her husband's personality, or her lack of knowledge, let's call it stupidity, play into her murderous decision?

Psychologists have said that sometimes in post-partum psychosis, women can have delusions about the baby or hallucinations, like hearing voices telling them to do certain things to harm the baby. LA County welfare officials had been repeatedly warned about the danger to the woman's children. A judge had awarded temporary custody to the father two months earlier.

What genetic or epigenetic influences might have played a part in the mother's psychotic-like behavior? Did post-partum depression play a part? Did her clear confession eliminate the possibility of a "temporary insanity" defense? Can psychologically normal people murder?

SOME PEOPLE THINK THEY KNOW EVERYTHING

While we are making great strides in understanding human behavior, there is so much we don't know. The certainty of our beliefs in so many areas, hobbles our individual progress-- and the progress of our society. This week Arkansas passed a bill in their House, 72-21, to allow creationism to be taught is schools. There is no empirical evidence for creationism, all the evidence is for the "Big

Bang" --then evolution. The same week, a governor in Pakistan amended the law, so that now, all university students must take a course in the Qur'an. Both governments are certain that they are right, and that all students must have identities that reflect the values of those who govern them. But which government is right? Or, are they both wrong?

Can science ever overcome superstition and the tradition of three millennia of the mythical or actual Moses? His memory is primary for the Jews, and is extremely important for the Christians and Muslims.

Most of us have accepted as fundamental elements of our identities ideas we have heard: at mother's knee; from our teachers; from our political, or would be, leaders; from social media; and from any number of other sources seeking to get us to believe or follow. Is capitalism really the best economic system? Is the welfare state really the best social program? Is the party platform of the Democrats really the best for the country? Is evangelical Christianity really what Jesus proposed? Is a democratic republic really the best for of government? Is "let the buyer beware" the best model for the commercial aspect of a society?

So many questions! Should we believe every propagandist of governmental ideas, every sect or religion, every ad we see on television? Should we think through and analyze the beliefs that make up our identities? Should we accept every pronouncement of QAnon< just because he wrote it? As a Catholic, do you believe everything the Pope says? In 2021 many American bishops wanted to deny Communion to those who would allow abortion, like the American President, but the Pope disagreed. My goodness!, will I be forced to think my way to a justifiable identity?

Let's take a look at the identities of those Alabama lawmakers. They are typical of so many Americans who believe intently, but have seldom examined their beliefs.

HAVE THE LAWMAKERS READ AND UNDERSTOOD THEIR SCRIPTURES AND THE QUESTIONS SURROUNDING THEM?

Let's look for a moment at the foundations of the Judeo-Christian religions and question whether some people with very strong Christian identities have actually investigated their fundamental scriptures and the history behind them. Admittedly religions are based on faith--but is there a factual or philosophical insight that is believable? When the Buddha said, "If you want to be happy, eliminate your desires." That might certainly be possible for some people. Certainly, having your desires unfulfilled might make your own happiness harder to come by! So a key Buddhist belief makes sense. But isn't it un-American to not want more and more?

So, what about: angels delivering messages, a terrible Hell built by a loving and merciful God, popes changing God's ideas to follow theirs, (Matthew 18:18, "Truly I tell you, whatever you bind on earth will be bound in heaven, and whatever you loose on earth will be loosed in heaven.")

But the story of Moses and Judeo-Christian Scriptures are the foundation for the stated religious values of more than 56% of the world's population—all following the religion attributed by Moses to beginning with Abraham, in Genesis Chapter 22. The Ten Commandments, and other aspects of Mosaic law, were the reason that Jesus preached—"to fulfill the law." (Matthew 5:17) Of course, most Christian religions have gone well beyond seeing Jesus as a prophet—now seeing him as God. The Muslims see both Moses and Jesus as among the five major prophets (Abraham, Noah, Moses, Jesus, and Mohammad)—but Mohammad is the last, and most important.

Many people believe that the Bible was written by people who were observing the events at the time. The truth is that both the New Testament and the Old Testament (Tanakh) were written long after the events actually happened, if they happened at all. So they are not historical documents, they are theological. The only written evidence comes hundreds of years after the events were supposedly originally chronicled.

If Abraham lived about 1800 BC, as some people think, and Moses lived about 600 years later, how might Moses have known about Abraham, unless God told him. Since Moses did talk to God (from the burning bush in Exodus 3 and on Sinai in Exodus and Deuteronomy), so possibly God did tell him.

Supposedly, Moses wrote the first 5 books of the Bible. In what language were they written? Written Hebrew is first known to have been used 300 to 400 years after Moses lived. If Moses grew up in Egypt, as we are told, the books may have been written in Egyptian hieroglyphics. However if he was as educated as some believe, they could have been written in Phoenician. Possibly, they were not actually written but were handed down orally—possibly by a number of poets and storytellers.

The Bible tells us that Moses's mother put him in a basket, sealed it with pitch (tar) and floated it through the reeds of the river. (Exodus 2:1-5) There he was picked up by an Egyptian princess and raised to adulthood. There is a similar story that was circulated about 500 years later, that the great King Sargon, who had actually lived a thousand years before Moses, had written an autobiography, which surfaced about 700 BCE. The story was that Sargon's mother had put him in a basket sealed with pitch, floated it among the reeds of the river, where he was eventually picked up by a gardener and raised. Did the oral transmission of the Bible adopt and adapt the story of Sargon and apply it to Moses, or did the supposed autobiography pick up the story of Moses and incorporate it into the long dead king's autobiography? Did either happen? Did neither happen?

Eventually we discovered the Dead Sea Scrolls, which were written from about 400 BCE to 300 AD. They were written in Hebrew, Greek and Aramaic. Many of the books of the Bible are represented in the scrolls. So our only written evidence of the Old Testament comes to us a thousand years after Moses began to write it.

Similarly, the New Testament began to tell the story of Jesus about 25 or 30 years after he had died in about 30 A.D. Mark was the first gospel written. This was about one lifetime removed from the death of Jesus.

Lifespans of Jews in First Century Rome, determined by examining hundreds of bodies in Roman catacombs were 22 to 25 years. Estimates of Galilean farmers at that time was about 29 years. Jesus was 33 when he died, according to the New Testament. If Mark's gospel was written in about 55, it was about one lifetime after Jesus lived. Matthew and Luke were written about two lifetimes after Jesus lived, and John's gospel, written about 75 years after Jesus died, is about two and a half lifetimes removed from the time of Jesus's death. And as religious scholars have observed, Jesus becomes more God-like with each succeeding gospel.

All Biblical scholars know that neither Paul, nor the gospel writers, the Evangelists, had ever met Jesus--so the eye-witness accounts that we are all familiar with, were never witnessed by those who wrote about them. And, we don't have their original writings. A few bits of papyrus with some of the gospel's texts are dated 60 to 100 years after the original Greek texts were written.

The oldest complete texts (codices) of the Evangelists, so far found, are the Codex Sinaiticus, copied by three or four monks about 300 years after the originals were written, and the Codex Vaticanus, written by two scribes, a few years earlier. Researchers have found well over 20,000 corrections and additions in these codices. So the original codices, written several lifetimes after the first were written may have been changed to fit Fourth Century theology. For example, Mark's account of Mary Magdalene's Sunday visit to the tomb of Jesus did not say he had risen from the dead--as the later gospel of Matthew did. So Mark's gospel was changed to correspond to Matthew's.

As Biblical scholars and Alabama legislators know, the world was created in 4004 BCE. The 17th Century's Anglican Bishop Ussher had meticulously calculated it, using the Biblical ages of men like Methuselah, Noah and Adam--all over 900 years-old. Then there were lots of "begats" noting who was born to whom. Liberal Biblical scholars see that date as mythologically interesting, Alabama lawmakers seem to see it as fact.

Using Ussher's calculations, Noah's flood was about 2450 BCE. There are many flood myths from our multi-cultural past. We find them inundating every continent and most islands. In fact, flood myths are "a dime a dousing." Many in the Abrahamic religions seem to know only the story of Noah, and his ark that couldn't possibly hold all of the flora and fauna of the world. With 5400 species of mammals, 10,000 species of birds, and another 10,000 species of reptiles, there wouldn't have been room for Noah and his family. If he had merely frozen the fertilized ova of his macrocosmic menagerie, it might have been possible, but the ark's arctic possibilities were minimal--being in the warm Mideast. And we might note that there is no evidence for a worldwide flood--especially in the last 20,000 years!

There is a more than slight possibility that the mythical flood of Noah was really a retelling of the mythical flood of Gilgamesh. The semi-divine king of Uruk who experienced a great flood about the year 2700 BCE. The story was written about 1800 BCE, fragments of the story are found in clay tablets from 4000 years ago. The more complete story is from about 1100 BCE. So, at every stage it pre-dates Noah and his ark.

Back to the New Testament. Paul was probably born in 5 to 15 AD, so was 10 to 20 years younger than Jesus who was probably born in 4 to 6 BCE. Matthew and Luke say that Jesus was born at the time of King Herod--and Herod died in 4 BCE.

Paul wrote his letters (epistles) from about 50 to 68 AD, from the time he was 35 to 45 years old until he was 52 to 62. The earliest copies are from about 200 AD.

Tradition has Paul and Peter being martyred by Nero, who blamed Rome's fire on the Christians. This martyrdom would have happened in 64 AD when the fire died. But Paul's epistle, 2 Timothy, was apparently written in 68 AD. Nero committed suicide in June of 68 AD. Was he sad because he had killed Paul? Had he ever caught Paul? Was it just a good story?

So a number of "truths" from the Bible may be questioned, unless you are a legislator from the deep South. But American religious beliefs seem to be pragmatically flexible rather than permanently fixed!

A Pew Research poll from January 2021 found that the pandemic made Americans' religious beliefs stronger, more than in any developed country. 30% of Americans increased their belief. But 6 months later, a Gallop poll found that only 16% of Americans believed that the influence of religion was increasing, but 82% found it decreasing. And the number of churchgoers is now below 50%.

Disasters increase religiosity. When your priest, president or imam cannot undo a war, earthquake, flood or famine there is no other option than to pray. So religious beliefs are an essential part of the identities of many, if not most, of the world's population.

Look at the last few minutes of a situation--and you know the whole story. Very true, if your are a simpleton!

Liz Cheney was ousted from the third most important position in the House Republican Party in ay of 2021. She was replaced by Elise Stefanik. Cheney voted with Trump 93% of the time, while Stefanik voted with him 78% of the time, according to one conservative evaluation group, while the American Conservative Union had Liz at a 78% rating and Elise at 44%. But the question is "What have you done lately?" Liz voted to impeach Trump for his role in the January 6th invasion of the Capitol. Elise didn't. Liz voted to affirm the clear election of Joe Biden. Elise didn't. Elise backed Trump's lie that the election was stolen from him--even though in Trump's 60 plus court actions to overturn the election, he could not offer any evidence to support his case--even in courts where he had appointed the judge. Trump loyalists accepted his word without any evidence. But most in Trump's party accepted his word over the evidence. Should we look at the whole voting record, or only the last two votes?

We see the last 9 minutes of George Floyd's life and his death, and he becomes an international icon. We forget that we say we are a nation of laws, and he broke several and refused to get into the police car. Yes, he was killed by the police officer, apparently unintentionally. Yes, the punishment didn't fit the crime. Should we look at the last half hour of his life, or the last 15 years, or only the last nine minutes?

Should we look with sadness at Napoleon's last years and death on St. Helena. He had given us the important Napoleonic code of laws. Or should we remember the millions who died because of his ambition?

Should we look only at Mother Theresa's recent saintliness, or the hundred of years of Crusades, the Inquisitions, and the thousands of sexually abuse children in Ireland, Canada and the U.S., in evaluating her church?

Is all of truth captured in the last minute? Or must we look at the whole of history to have a better glimpse of truth?

WHOSE LAND IS IT ANYWAY?

Why is the accident of birth the major determinant of life? If my father was a farmer in Senegal will I have the same opportunities as if by father was a billionaire Wall Street investor? My parents and their homeland determine 99.999999% of my opportunities in life.

If I had been born in San Francisco in the year 2000, why do I have more rights to the land than the Mexicans who had owned it before 1850, or the Native Americans who had owned it for 10,000 years before that. If I was a Jew born in Jerusalem, why do I have more rights than the Arabs who had populated Palestine for over a thousand years, the Romans who had owned it before that, the Egyptians, the Canaanites or any other group that has owned or controlled the area before and after it was an Israelite kingdom. The political answer is that "might makes right." But how does that comport with Kant's dictum that "we should treat everyone as ends in themselves, not a means only." To that we may add the nearly universal highly esteemed emotion of "empathy."

CHAPTER 4   OUR IDENTITIES--HOW WE CHOOSE AND USE VALUES AND EVIDENCE

Our identities, our celf-concepts and self-esteem. (see Volume I, Chapter 12), are essential for our psychological well-being. They should give us a perception of power that is necessary to handle our psychological inferiorities. Our identities can be based on a combination of:

- ➢ Our severe psychological problems—like narcissism or depression,
- ➢ Our present psychological needs and drives,
- ➢ The verifiable or faulty information that we have ingested,
- ➢ The values that we discussed earlier –self-centered, God-based, and society-based,
- ➢ Our successes and failures in life,
- ➢ The goals and objectives that we are willing to devote our lives to.

But our identities may not be based on highly probable facts or well-considered values, but are most often based on our present psychological needs. At the time of this writing, two glaring illustrations of out-of-the-ordinary identities emerged. One was the storming of the U.S. Capitol by hundreds of Americans who believed Donald Trump's false claim that he had been cheated out of the election. They also believed him, when he said he would march with them to the Capitol. The other prime example of identities on display was the Oprah Winfrey interview with Prince Harry and his wife, Meghan Markle.

So let's look at these illustrations in order to make us think more deeply about our own identities, where we are, how we have changed, and how we might intelligently evaluate and adjust our own identities as we navigate the river of life. It is obvious that the identity we had as a 5-year-old had changed considerably by the time we were 18. And, our identity has changed many times since--hopefully the changes were positive. But as we know all too well, some people have changed their identities negatively: some chose violent gang membership, some chose drug addiction, some gave up living and chose suicide. But, most of us have accepted socially approved identities of various sorts.

Truly, the experience of life can be marvelous or mad—and by using our intelligence and verifiable knowledge we can construct realistic identities with the increased likelihood of positive outcomes for our lives.

As we address a number of pressing problems for our times, which is the major goal of the next volume, we will be to see how our own identities will look at solutions for a societal problem—and we should be able to see how people with othcr idcntities may view the scene through quite different lenses. While we may approach a problem by mounting our chargers powered by different values, we should arm ourselves for the joust with weapons of psychological soundness, sharpened with the most probable and empirical evidence available. It is sad today, that so few people use the lances of logic in their battle for life—so many are dueling with pillows of propaganda. As comfortable as pillows are for napping, realistic identities must be forged and tempered with the mental metal of psychological soundness and philosophical sagacity.

So, in preparing for our journey through the human hurdles that the Fates have erected in our pursuit of utopia, let's glance at some present-day realities in the hope that we can clarify our own identities—and examine them.

PATHOLOGICAL IDENTITIES

Psychological problems may result in our adopting identities such as: Napoleon, God, or a famous athlete. While it is not uncommon to occasionally daydream about such identities, when such delusions of grandeur become all-important, we have a major psychological problem.

Narcissism, such as Donald Trump has consistently shown, is becoming a much more common psychological problem as we attempt to crawl out of our psychological holes of inferiority, that began in our infancy, and attempt to show that we are superior, (See Volume I, Chapters 11, 12, 14) as can be seen in the statements of Donald Trump, the narcissist can never admit anything that reduces his feelings of superiority.

News agencies counted 30,000 lies that he had told during his presidency. Many of those untruths were not actually lies but were rationalizations that his mind contrived to attempt to explain situations in which he would've been seen as inferior or wrong. As mentioned earlier, when one tells a lie, he knows that it is not true. When one rationalizes, he thinks that it is true. So when one has done something wrong, the mentally healthy person who has real self-esteem will tell the truth. People who have problems with their self-esteem may lie. But people who have mental problems are more likely to rationalize by finding reasons that sound plausible to them, but are actually false. Kellyanne Conway, one of President Trump's closest advisors, called these rationalizations "alternate truths." "Alternative truth" is like saying that to 2 + 2 =5,000!

But Trump was not the only man to want to rule forever! There's Putin, Modi in India, Alexander Lukashenko in Belarus, and leaders in Hungary, Poland, Rwanda, Indonesia, and most African and many South America countries. Their power ambitions lead to their controlling of both free speech and freedom of the press. We find such all-powerful, omniscient attitudes commonly in our world: "I am the boss." "I'm your father," "I'm your mother." And so, and so, and so!

NARCISISM—A PSYCHOLOGIAL INFLATION OF ONE'S IDENTITY

The Diagnostic and Statistical Manual of Mental Disorders of the American Psychiatric Association, (5th edition) lists nine symptoms for narcissism. A person who has five is considered to be narcissistic. Trump had all nine—and he was not the only national leader so afflicted. The list of symptoms is:

1. Has a grandiose sense of self-importance (e.g. exaggerates achievements and talents, expects to be recognized as superior without commensurate achievements).

2. Is preoccupied with fantasies of unlimited success, power, brilliance, beauty, or ideal love.

3. Believes that they are "special" and unique and can only be understood by, or should associate with, other special or high-status people (or institutions).

4. Requires excessive admiration.

5.   Has a sense of entitlement (i.e., unreasonable expectations of especially favorable treatment or automatic compliance with their expectations).

6.   Is interpersonally exploitative (i.e., takes advantage of others to achieve their own ends).

7.   Lacks empathy: is unwilling to recognize or identify with the feelings and needs of others.

8.   Is often envious of others or believes that others are envious of them.

9.   Shows arrogant, haughty behaviors or attitudes.

At the same time, people with a narcissistic personality disorder have trouble handling anything they perceive as criticism.

In 1964 Barry Goldwater ran for President against Lyndon Johnson. Fact magazine sent out 12,000 questionnaires to psychiatrists asking whether Goldwater was psychologically fit to be president. Nearly 2,500 were returned. About 45% said he was not fit, some said there wasn't enough information, others believed him fit. Some comments:

➢   "I believe Goldwater to be suffering from a chronic psychosis," wrote one.

➢   "A megalomaniacal, grandiose omnipotence appears to pervade Mr. Goldwater's personality giving further evidence of his denial and lack of recognition of his own feelings of insecurity and ineffectiveness," wrote another.

➢   "From his published statements I get the impression that Goldwater is basically a paranoid schizophrenic who decompensates from time to time. He resembles Mao Tse-tung," said a third.

➢   Not wanting to exclude other relevant 20th-century tyrants, another claimed, "I believe Goldwater has the same pathological makeup as Hitler, Castro, Stalin, and other known schizophrenic leaders."

The American Psychiatric Association (APA) then made a rule that their members should not evaluate people's mental health unless they had examined them personally. However, there are other associations of behavioral therapists that do not have such a rule. Observing people, such as through two-way mirrors is a standard technique in some therapeutic situations—because a therapist must understand the problem before a treatment regime can be developed. Donald Trump, having been in the public's eyes for years, along with the many books written about him by intimates, including a niece who is a licensed clinical psychologist, give us more than enough information to clearly diagnose him as having an advanced level of the narcissistic personality disorder.

OUR IDENTITIES AS A SOURCE OF OUR VALUES

In Volume I, Chapters 12 and 30, we discussed how and why identities develop. The major reasons are related to our need to feel power in our lives are often due to our not having been effectively loved as a child. This is often amplified by epigenetic abnormalities.

As you remember, power can come from having "power over" somebody or something or from having "power to" do something.

Self-centered identities, in most of us, can be seen from the time we are small children and throughout our lives. In school you may be a: smart student, nerd, cheerleader, football player, popular person, member of a well-thought-of club. As we age, our identities can change many times. It may be being: a father, a mother, a Porsche owner, rich, the owner of the big house, a millionaire, a scientist, a logical thinker, gang member, a boss, homeless, a pedophile, voyeur, or an unimportant failure.

God-based values may give us identities such as: Catholic, Jew, an Ultra-Orthodox Jew, Methodist, Shia, Sunni, priest, minister, rabbi, mullah, Pope, Bishop, evangelical, anti-abortion, yogi, monk, missionary, born again, ISIS, Al Qaeda, Mormon, Jehovah's Witnesses, Smith's Friends, Scientologist.

Society-based identities might be: police officer, teacher, firefighter, Democrat, Republican, Libertarian, Congressman, environmentalist, politician, King, Prime Minister—and recently in America, pro-Trump or anti-Trump.

A person may have a number of sub-identities at the same time—so one's "identity" becomes more complicated. For example, a woman might be: mother, Porsche owner, Democrat, Jewish, and teacher. Each of these identities may be more. or less, important. to her. So, to one person, being a millionaire may be more important than being a Lutheran. Being pro-Trump was often more important than family loyalties.

When we look at political identities, which have become primary for many, these last few years—often splitting friends and families who have adopted the "wrong" identity. A prime example is former Senate majority leader Mitch McConnell, who voted against the conviction of Donald Trump on the impeachment charge that Trump had inspired the invasion of the Capitol. He then immediately, minutes after the acquittal, called Trump, "practically and morally responsible" for his supporters' deadly attack on the Capitol.

In his speech he said, "President Trump is still liable for everything he did while he was in office as an ordinary citizen, he didn't get away with anything--YET." Then he continued, "Falsehoods by the most powerful man on earth because he was angry, he had lost an election. Former President Trump's actions preceded the riot for a disgraceful — disgraceful dereliction of duty. . . There's no question, none, that President Trump is practically and morally responsible for provoking the events of the day. No question about it. The people that stormed this building believed they were acting on the wishes and instructions of their president. . . . . It was also the entire manufactured atmosphere of looming catastrophe, the increasingly wild myths — myths about Democratic landslide election that was somehow being stolen, some secret coup by our now-President. Now, I defended the President's rights to bring any complaints to our legal system. The legal system spoke. The Electoral College spoke. . . These criminals were carrying his banners, hanging his flags, and screaming their loyalty to him. It was obvious that only President Trump could end this. He was the only one who could. Former aides publicly begged him to do so. Loyal allies frantically called the administration. The President did not act swiftly. He did not do his job. He didn't take steps so federal law could be faithfully executed and order restored. No. Instead, according to public reports, he watched television happily — happily as the chaos unfolded. He kept pressing his scheme to overturn the election."

McConnell chastised Trump for not doing his Constitutional duty and said he could be taken to criminal court. Then, a few weeks later, he said that if Trump were nominated in 2024, he would "absolutely" support him.   America first or the party first? Values and identity are inseparable.

It is not surprising to find narcissism among leaders at every level of our societies. It seems to afflict men far more than women. Is it genetic, epigenetic, or merely more often tolerated in men? After all, white male privilege allows all sorts of irrational behavior!

THE CAPITOL INVADERS

It's not possible to analyze the invaders, like it is to analyze Trump, with his years of public presence and public utterances. But various crashers of the Capitol thought of themselves in idealized terms as "patriots." They were taking back the government that had been stolen from them by the unidentified and invisible demons of election fraud.

We did see the power drives uncovered as the psychological inferiority complexes were assuaged and several "patriots" mounted the podium hill of the House of Representatives and sat in the Speaker's chair. No one was prouder of his accomplishment than the patriot who broke into Nancy Pelosi's office and was photographed with his feet on her desk. But, within days he was jailed and charged with Federal felonies. Did his revolutionary identity bring him the lasting fame of a Washington or Jefferson? Hardly!

The psychological insufficiencies of these patriots were evident in their actions. Building a gallows in front of the Capitol to hang Mike Pence, the President's right hand man for four years because he couldn't do what he was powerless to do—overturn the election, that Joe Biden had won by seven million votes. Hundreds of times that afternoon, the psychological insufficiencies of the rioters, egged on by the fraudulent identity-building of Trump, Fox and QAnon, led to the killing of six people, more than $30 million in damages, and an irreparable damage to the image of the modern home of democracy.

But the erroneous erection of lofty pseudo-identities of patriotism, powered by the fuel of inferiorities, will be cooled for many in the cells of federal prisons. Too bad that their identities were not grounded in fact and reality! Realistic intelligent identities would judiciously evaluate the past, the present, and the future!

MEGHAN AND HARRY

In the famous Oprah Winfrey interview with Prince Harry and Meghan Markle, the American and British "royals" identities were obvious in the post-interview reactions. The day before the interview, a British friend opined that the Americans would side with Meghan and the British population would mainly side with the Crown. And that's what happened, to a large degree. Meghan related that a member of the Royal Family was concerned that their baby would not have white skin. She also related how the tabloid press was continually hounding her and printed false information. The combination of pressures prompted serious thoughts of suicide. Harry, whose mother Princess Diana, was killed by the pursuit of the paparazzi, and who had had major depression issues because of it, sympathized with his wife. An outpouring of sympathy and concern erupted from the American audience. Surprisingly, many Brits agreed.

So we see Meghan's identity as a beautiful white actress, identified as black because there is an unwritten rule that one Black gene colors the entire genome. Her background as a middle-class Angelino with a Black mother who had earned a Master's degree from one of America's most prestigious universities, the University of Southern California. Meghan was raised in Windsor Hills, an upper-class area in Los Angeles. She graduated from one of the two top-rated Catholic high schools in Los Angeles, the same school where Walt Disney sent his daughter. Then she graduated from Northwestern University, rated the 24th best university in the U.S. of over 4,000 universities. Her identity should include the factors that she is very intelligent, as well as highly educated. So her identity can be seen as stellar up to the time that she became "a royal."

Harry's identity seems to have been slightly different from what the royal image-makers would have desired. As a teen, he was photographed smoking cannabis, then some years later, dancing nude at a party in Las Vegas. More important, he became a "real" soldier for a decade, serving tours in Afghanistan and rising in the officer ranks. It seems that he has followed his great uncle Edward VIII in renouncing the royal path—and even worse, marrying an American.

So, we have two strong-willed, intelligent, independent people cast into a royal role, but too far down the aristocratic pecking order to ever become a ruler—even if either actually aspired to the throne and its duties, which seems unlikely.

After the interview, some British newspapers and commentators saw it quite differently than the American media. The couple were attacking the monarchy—an unforgivable sin! They noted that the queen had spent $30 million on their wedding. What they didn't point out is how little the monarchy costs. Its yearly $85 million expenses are only about $1.25 per inhabitant of the UK. So it doesn't cost much to have a crowned head on hand, if you ever need one.

The royals are rich, but even if the royal family's total property value of $88 billion were equally divided among the population, each would receive only about $1250—one vacation in Greece or the Canaries, or a couple of weeks in a pub, and it would disappear! Might as well keep the royals— they are good press!

As we will soon point out, and as most you already know, a major logical fallacy is attacking the person, rather than the argument. Could the British commentators prove that no royal had commented on the skin color of the expected child? Could they prove that Meghan had never had suicidal urges? More than highly unlikely-- without a fly on the wall recording conversations on his tiny smart phone!

Identities often have deep roots. Many British republicans have tried for many years to eliminate the pomp and payroll of the Windsors. But tradition rules. And, America has its own traditions—low taxes, exemptions for all churches from taxation, "in God we trust" on its coins, and the right to own firearms.

MORE ON IDENTITIES

So we have billions of identities in our world, combinations of political, religious, economic, familial, geographical, racial, ethnic, recreational—and many more. No wonder we have so many differences in values and opinions.

Muslim women who want to wear the full body covering burka are running afoul of laws in many countries. Should they move back to Afghanistan?

Cowboys who want to carry holstered pistols in Texas, would be arrested in Europe—or about anyplace else in the civilized world!

Because there are so many identities and values, we can expect some real discord among people. But conflicts in values also occur within most people.

COGNITIVE DISSONANCE

Psychologists have realized for some time that our values, our beliefs and our ideas, often conflict. "Cognitive" means that we can think about something, but "dissonance" means the there are aspects of our thinking that are in conflict. That conflict may be a minor static, "I have to miss church today because I have to substitute at work." Or it may be a major dissonance, "I love my country and would fight for it, but I don't agree with this war, so I'm emigrating to Canada."

You can imagine the dissonance in Prince Harry's mind. His father was unfaithful to his mother. His mother was nurturing, his father-- emotionally distant. His brother, who had always been emotionally close, was now distant as their wives did not connect emotionally or culturally. His adult life had been military, not aristocratic. His wife was subject to the negative tabloid temperament that his mother hadn't faced, but the paparazzi pursued her with equal ferocity. With his own wife and family primary, must he cut the ties of royal tradition, of family friendships, of a cool crown? Seldom have any of our kind faced such dissonance. He chose his wife and family, and a very different lifestyle. And his new countrymen applauded.

How had the January 6th "patriots" fared? Living in a land of freedom that was won by armed rebellion, with a Constitution that guarantees liberty and the right to assemble, spurred on by reactionary pundits and false prophets of the social media, and led by the President of the country—what is there to fear? Without looking at the evidence that included: laws against insurrection, and absolutely no evidence for the conspiracies that were alleged by the unseen phantoms of the internet. (Yet, the right-leaning American Enterprise Institute's recent survey showed that 28% of white evangelicals believed QAnon.) The theory of cognitive dissonance recognizes that often people will follow an absolutely false solution if it seems the most appropriate or the simplest, and it develops or enhances an identity that will gain the approval of others.

Examples of conflicts were noted several times in the first volume. But let's look at some more conflicts in our more recent times. Back to Harry and Meghan. Harry certainly could blame the paparazzi for killing his mother. His wife was now subject to the same stresses. His relationship with his brother, Prince William, was strained. His father refused to answer his phone calls. So much for the prodigal son!

Our identities often have long tentacles. The House of Windsor is still reeling from Edward VIII's abdication to marry another American divorcee. But had he remained king and married a fertile English girl, Queen Elizabeth might only be cousin to whoever would be on the throne today. So the royals should be thankful that pre-owned American women tempt their royal rascals out of the line of succession! Edward would be so proud of Harry.

If we are to be "thinking" people, we should look deeply into why we hold the basic assumptions that we do. On analysis, I may find that my mother's deeply held religious assumption may not be as obvious as I believed when I was ten-years old. I may question my father's assumption that liberty is the major political ideal. His "dog eat dog" approach to economics may not always work best. And Uncle Charley's democratic ideals may be open to question.

Along with examining my basic assumptions, I might evaluate the evidence I am using to back up my assumptions.

On another tack. There are political and sociological studies that indicate the make-up of those who voted in the 2016 presidential election. For Trump there were educated and successful people who wanted lower taxes for their businesses or wanted to keep more of their pension checks. They blamed "big government" for the anti-capitalist pro-citizen rules that cut their profits. There were also rust-belt voters, often with educations of high school or less who were unemployed or considered themselves under-employed. They blamed immigration. There were also the anti-abortion voters who were generally evangelical Protestants or conservative Catholics. They blamed a godless government. Combined, they made up a conservative-reactionary bloc. These were rational value-based decisions. They could be seen as rational, though not universally agreed upon, values.

These "value desires" were combined, possibly even more importantly, with the strong, nearly universal, inferiority feelings that craved power to create, or bolster, their self-esteem. These psychologically-based motivations are not related to the intelligent concerns that modern democracies assume guide the marking of ballots.

This became evident early in the primaries when Trump used the fallacious logic of the "ad hominem" fallacy, in which a person attacks the speaker, rather than the argument. The lower one's logical knowledge, or the greater one's feelings of inferiority, the more effective this type of attack is. When confronted with Trump's deluge of delusions and lies, Hilary asked Michelle Obama how to handle it, Michelle said, "When they go low, we go high." But Barack Obama had faced two men of principle, in Mitt Romney and John McCain. Since the earliest days of the American republic, it has been common for each side to land some low blows—sometimes true, sometimes not. But Donald Trump's combination of severe narcissism, of which his lack of empathy is but one of the nine symptoms of his severe personality problem, and his cutthroat business methodology was a far different political opponent than has ever crossed the American political stage.

Trump called Ted Cruz "lying Ted," Marco Rubio "little Marco," Jeb Bush "low energy Jeb," Ben Carson "Sleepy Ben" (still later he named him Minister of Housing and Urban Development). He seldom criticized the positions of his Republican adversaries-- which were often similar to his.

After gaining the nomination, he continued his attacks on Hilary Clinton, as "Crooked Hilary" and "Lock her up." He did attack her in other ways, claiming that her emailing was flawed and that she was responsible for the death of her friend, the Ambassador in Benghazi. Evidence before and after the election showed that neither case was true. Then he settled on two phrases that few would disagree with: "Make America Great Again" and "America first." He didn't say what was wrong with America, except that it took in too many immigrants, especially Mexicans and Muslims—and chain migration, citizens bringing in relatives was an outrage. But there were not enough Slovenians in the U.S. so Melania's parents had no problems becoming residents and citizens.

Trump did indicate that the national debt was too high and that he should be able to eliminate it is eight years. Instead, he increased it by a third, $7 trillion, in four years. All Americans want their taxes reduced. So he gave huge permanent tax reductions to the rich and to corporations, and temporary reductions to the workers—so everybody was happy!

People with inferiority complexes, which covers just about all of us, want our fears diminished, our anger assuaged, and our hopes appeased. That's why, since Aristotle, and undoubtedly before, students of human nature have realized that, "men are ruled by imagination and emotion, not by reason."

Lawyers know this. There is an old mantra among attorneys that "if your client is not guilty-- go to a judge for the trial, if he is guilty--demand a jury trial." They know that playing on the emotions of the jurors usually wins-- telling them about the accused's abusive alcoholic parents or his being bullied at school, will outweigh, or at least lessen, his guilt for robbing a bank or murdering his parents. And, his experiences may have been critical in his value development. But will they persist if he is allowed back in society? Are his genes, that increase potential violence, still present? A "not guilty" verdict doesn't demethylate genes or erase unconscious propensities to violence. Is it fair to the accused criminal to punish him for epigenetic or unconscious tendencies to violence for which he was not responsible? But, is it fair to society to turn him loose? But who said that "things are always fair?"

We are seeing more liberal governors and district attorneys that want to reduce sentences and eliminate the death penalty, but many in the conservative electorate want the bad guys punished and kept out of their neighborhoods. Several "do gooders" have been subject to recall.

And, what if you want to run for a political office, appeal to the psychological natures of the electorate—not to their intellects. Their psychological needs, as values, will be primary. So promise a better job to minimize their economic fears. Promise to shut down immigration or to go to war with Iran to answer their anger. But most of all, promise fatter wallets, reduced taxes, and pie in the sky.

However, if developing the best country is the goal, we need people who are not hampered by genetic, epigenetic, or unconscious anchors to logical thinking. We need people who are educated in logic, world history and other important areas---and who have well-thought-out values.

The people with immature identities were attracted to Trump in his earlier rallies. He gave them so many people to feel superior to: Lyin' Ted, Little Marco, Crooked Hillary, drug-dealing raping Mexicans, and of course the Muslims. Then when his hand-picked cabinet secretaries and top aides quit his administration, he was generous with his vitriol on their departure. He was particularly angry when Rex Tillerson, his Secretary of State, had referred to him as a "moron." When he cancelled a visit to the American war-dead at the American cemetery near Paris because it had started raining, he said, "those Americans who had died in the war were losers and suckers." He had said similar things about fellow Republican, and war hero, John McCain. But Trumps was never a sucker. He avoided Vietnam when his father convinced a doctor-friend to write that Donald had a heel spur. According to the New York Times and Newsweek, in 2018, the podiatrist, Larry Braunstein, who lived in one of Donald's fathers apartments, did a favor for Trump by writing that Donald's heel spurs would make it impossible for him to serve. The Army, without x-raying, bought the story. And although 10% of people have heel spurs, according to the Cleveland Clinic, they don't keep most of us out of the service. The doctor's daughters reported that Trump had no heel spurs. (Mine didn't give me any trouble until twenty years after my discharge!)

It does wonders for immature egos when they can follow a President who continually vomits sarcasms and derisions against competent people. Just think of how many generals, senators, and business leaders they can now feel superior to. Their artificially inflated identities will follow the piper--whether he is leading rats or lemmings. It feels so good to feel important--even if you didn't earn it!

But it is not just the average Joe or Josephine that is caught up with solidifying their identity by following an important leader, no matter how deranged. Aspiring politicians hitch their wagons to leaders, no matter where they are leading their country. Napoleon, Putin, Trump, Xi and Kim have all exuded power. For those whose identities yearn for power--follow those with proven power.

We can see the coattails of Trump and his downplaying of the pandemic when we look at the number of Republican governors who led their citizens to the coroner. Note also the education rankings of the states and their pandemic death rates.

STATES RANKED BY

1.	North Dakota — 13,194 per 100,000 population	R	14
2.	South Dakota — 12,858 per 100,000	R	25
3.	Rhode Island — 12,203 per 100,000	D	27
4.	Utah — 11,738 per 100,000	R	18
5.	Arizona — 11,373 per 100,000	R	49
6.	Tennessee — 11,294 per 100,000	R	35
7.	Oklahoma — 10,853 per 100,000	R	47
8.	Iowa — 10,805 per 100,000	R	23
9.	Arkansas — 10,782 per 100,000	R	42
10.	Wisconsin — 10,690 per 100,000	D	8
11.	Nebraska — 10,536 per 100,000	R	11
12.	Kansas — 10,281 per 100,000	D	29
13.	South Carolina — 10,242 per 100,000	R	43
14.	Alabama — 10,210 per 100,000	R	44
15.	Mississippi — 10,013 per 100,000	R	46
16.	Indiana — 9,975 per 100,000	R	15
17.	Idaho — 9,732 per 100,000	R	38
18.	Nevada — 9,639 per 100,000	D	45
19.	Illinois — 9,507 per 100,000	D	1
20.	Wyoming — 9,498 per 100,000	R	19
21.	Montana — 9,471 per 100,000	R	26
22.	Georgia — 9,431 per 100,000	R	34
23.	Louisiana — 9,356 per 100,000	D	49
24.	Texas — 9,330 per 100,000	R	28
25.	Missouri — 9,311 per 100,000	R	36
26.	Kentucky — 9,298 per 100,000	D	16
27.	New Jersey — 9,221 cases per 100,000	D	3
28.	California — 9,130 per 100,000	D	37
29.	Delaware — 9,107 per 100,000	D	9
30.	Florida — 9,092 per 100,000	R	22
31.	New Mexico — 8,930 per 100,000	D	50
32.	New York — 8,776 per 100,000	D	12
33.	Minnesota — 8,727 per 100,000	D	7
34.	Massachusetts — 8,612 per 100,000	R	1
35.	Ohio — 8,398 per 100,000	R	32
36.	North Carolina — 8,396 per 100,000	D	30
37.	Alaska — 8,106 per 100,000	R	48
38.	Connecticut — 8,082 per 100,000	D	2
39.	Colorado — 7,649 per 100,000	D	17
40.	Pennsylvania — 7,485 per 100,000	D	24
41.	West Virginia — 7,469 per 100,000	R	39

42.	Virginia — 6,890 per 100,000	D	4
43.	Michigan — 6,608 per 100,000	D	33
44.	Maryland — 6,432 per 100,000	R	10
45.	New Hampshire — 5,682 per 100,000	R	6
46.	Washington — 4,586 per 100,000	D	2
47.	Oregon — 3,747 per 100,000	D	40
48.	Maine — 3,426 per 100,000	D	20
49.	Vermont — 2,610 per 100,000	D	5
50.	Hawaii — 1,971 per 100,000	D	31

Oh well, being dead is preferable to changing parties!

Our identities are so often so deeply ingrained in us, that we assume that all intelligent people the world over, agree with us. What a mistake! We start with different basic assumptions, our sources of evidence, like social media or an informed press are different, our political and economic systems are different, and we worship gods with different names—Deus, Allah, Brahma or cash. Can our various identities, assumptions, and our choices of evidence, ever share the same stage, the same cage, or the same pulpit? Not yet. But effective education is an essential starting line.

LOVE AND POWER IN FORMING IDENTITIES

Hopefully, Volume One was clear in illustrating how genetics may give many of us the bases of our behavior. Until recently, psychologists followed John Locke's idea that we are born with minds that are blank slates, not written on until we were born. Freud's therapies assumed this. But if animals have instincts, and if we are animals, we probably have them too. Then we have had the theological influences that we are made in the Image of God--and there is no evidence that God has instincts! Looking at Robert Ardrey's research assembled in his books, "African Genesis" and "The Territorial Imperative" we can see a great deal of evidence that many animals have instincts for power, often exhibited as violence. So, we undoubtedly have instincts. Then we add the epigenetic changes to our genes from ancestors, our epigenetic changes from our life in the womb, then our early childhood experiences, then later life experiences--then we have US!

PARENTS

Our parents unknowingly, or uncaringly, pass on genetic and epigenetic traits. They then may do their best to meet our physiological and psychological needs. They may feed us nourishing diets, see that we exercise adequately, and keep or social media and video game involvement to under 40 hours a week! But hugging is so important. Warm physical contact usually releases the hormone oxytocin.

CHAPTER 5   VALIDATING IDENTITIES—HOW DO WE KNOW WHAT WE KNOW?

The next concern is how do we know what we know? In philosophy this is called the area of epistemology. How do we know something? Did we arrive at a belief on our own? Did someone tell us? Do we remember something from the past that had elicited this belief? Are we skeptical of what others believe? Have we arrived at our own beliefs through observation – such as living in Sweden for several years, in the UK for several years, and the USA for several years? This would give us more evidence about some societies than if we just traveled in each country for a week, or read about each country in a magazine.

A major question has been whether reasoning (rationalism), is more important than observing and experimenting (empiricism). Until recently, the idea of being an empiricist in the rationalistic world of religion, could get you burned at the stake.

Giordano Bruno was a 16th Century Dominican priest, philosopher, mathematician and theorist of cosmology. He had the absurd idea that the stars were actually suns surrounded by their own planets. He even thought that some of these had planets might possess life forms. Even more absurd were his disbeliefs of the Catholic doctrines of: eternal damnation in hell, the Trinity, and the virginity of Mary the mother of Jesus. He also had some other beliefs that were more akin to Hinduism than to Catholicism. The Inquisitional courts in Venice and Rome found him guilty of heresy against the church. So naturally, he was burned at the stake after first being hung upside down while naked.

Serves him right! Science has no place in a world of myth!

Religions are always rationalistic, and theologians use their imaginations to understand and complicate the usually simple moral ideas of their religion's founder. Political systems may suffer similar irrationalities. So people may curse the socialism of the USSR and Cuba, envy that of China's economic successes, and hope to duplicate the socialistic welfare states of the Nordic countries. But in comparing socialistic welfare systems, they have hard evidence—the evidence of empiricism.

Karl Marx, in developing his theory of communism used both empirical thinking and rationalistic thinking. The capitalists truly exploited their workers. There was enough money, but it was not distributed equitably. So from his desk in the reading room of the British Museum, he theorized a utopia in which all toiled equally hard and shared the fruits of their labor equally. He admitted that society would first have to become socialistic, where people could reap the fruits of their labor, without the capitalists taking most. But eventually it will be, "From each according to his ability, to each according to his needs." What a lovely thought! The problem is that people are not physically or mentally equal---and they don't have equal work ethics. Still more important--they are selfishly self-centered.

The failures of his system, as shown in the USSR, was in attempting to put into a real society, ideas that were developed using reason alone, springing from society-based assumptions. In the real world, the self-centered values of people in the USSR, could not be realized in the Soviet socialistic model. On the other hand, the Nordic Model of a welfare state, partially funded by state capitalism, has produced the world's happiest and honest people and a higher median salary than the U.S.—and more billionaires per million people!

There are a number of Communist parties in the world, but there are no communist nations. Several have tried socialism. The USSR and Cuba failed miserably. China has had great economic success, but personal liberties are often trampled in the autocrat-led march toward socialism.

The Nordic countries have been able to have both a high level of freedom and a high level of welfare--"to each according to his need." So Marx attempted to equalize our values and identities. Too bad that he didn't have the benefit of knowing the psychological work of Freud and Adler, the epigenetic findings of today's researchers, and a crystal ball to see 175 years into the future! His beliefs, while ideologically and economically important, have yet to follow the dialectic that he assumed.

WE OFTEN ACCEPT EVIDENCE, TRUE OR FALSE, IF IT REINFORCES OUR IDENTITY

There is often a huge chasm between our "true beliefs," which we think are true knowledge, and that of empirical knowledge that has been tested, re-tested and verified. In science we say that it has reached a high degree of probability. The sciences are not equally verifiable. The more variables in the study, the less probable the conclusion. The more difficult it is to measure the item being studied, the less probable the results of the study. If I am measuring the speed of light, and have an accurate gauge, my results should be highly probable. But, if I study 10,000 soldiers in a test on sexual harassment, then pick out just one soldier, he may be more or less of a harasser thar the average of the study shows. In fact, he may not be a harasser at all. It is possible that he is one who has been harassed!!

So scientists the world over, who measure the speed of light with accurate gauges, have a high probability of having the same result. But measuring intelligence throughout the world with different tests by psychologists, or assessing sexual violence with different criteria by sociologists in various countries, have far too many variables to determine a universal finding. So, if we hear that one racial, ethnic or religious group is more intelligent or more violent than another, we might question some conclusions. But the major problem we see today, is in hearing or reading information that is totally false—without any evidence at all! But it commonly becomes the "true" beliefs of the people whose identities are validated by that evidence.

➤ If you die as a male suicide bomber of infidels, you go immediately to Paradise and will enjoy the adoration of 72 virgins. While the Koran does not promise this, some theologians do.

➤ Female suicide bombers are promised beauty and a faithful husband.

➤ The popes promised heaven to the Crusaders.

➤Leaders of countries entice their young warriors to fight with pride for their countries.

➤Stock brokers promise wealth to their customers.

➤Young lovers promise each other eternal bliss.

But what are the realities? No one has seen Paradise. But since we don't want to die, the hope of a happy afterlife sounds tempting. That is why so many religions flourish. The religions of Abraham promise us a happy place. Hinduism says if we are really good, and enlightened, we can disappear and leave this ugly temporal world. Some religions allow us to be spirits that live just beyond this world.

The warriors who return are given medals. The stock traders may or may not make you money. And, half of the young lovers will eventually divorce. (Divorce rates are going down in America—because fewer are getting married, so when they split, it is not a recorded divorce.) So, promises don't provide certainty, in fact they may be totally false, but they enhance our identities and increase our self-esteem.

So our psychological set is primary. Truth, as many see it, is only that which builds on our primary psychological needs, not that which corresponds to empirical or historical evidence. And in a democracy "I am entitled to my own opinions!" And, as they say, I am entitled to my own alternative facts! Who cares, as long as my identity is fertilized with the manure of misrepresentations.

When important people say things, most people will believe them. Whether it is the President of the United States, the Pope or bishops, members of their own political party, their parents, or their friends.

The point is—that when Donald Trump, Sean Hannity, Tucker Carlson, the recently deceased Rush Limbaugh, or any other radio or TV hosts or a QAnon post agrees with you--it affirms your identity. More than affirming it, it may be forming it. If you are uneducated, you probably have few relevant facts against which to measure other opinions or purported facts, such as one hears from the commentators on the right or left. If people were interested in believing more probable evidence, they could view many news channels--Fox News, CNN, BBC, and Al Jazeera. Of course, there are also the Russian and Chinese propaganda programs. But even they give you better information than Rush or Sean did!

DONALD TRUMP BECAME A MASTER IDENTITY CREATOR

In attempting to convince people to vote for him in the 2016 primaries and presidential election, then again in 2020--and continuing today--Donald Trump made promises, attacked everyone who didn't praise him, and lauded law and order and the sanctity of fertilized ova. He could not have predicted in early 2016 how he would create a national identity in which his narcissistic personality would be elevated beyond reality. The strength of the Trump-identity erected an opposite identity of equal strength. Families split, fights erupted in bars, citizens threw their hats into the ring of potential legislators, and Trumpers invaded the Capitol. An unprecedented outcome!

A number of authoritative books have been written about Donald Trump. Probably the best was written by his niece, Mary Trump, who is also a clinical psychologist. "Too Much and Never Enough: How My Family Created the World's Most Dangerous Man," shows how Trump's obvious personality problems had been encouraged by his sociopathic millionaire father and others. "Fear: Trump in the Whitehouse," by the esteemed journalist, Bob Woodward, is based on lengthy interviews with Trump and his aids. There are many negative facts, but the readers must make up their own minds. "Fire and Fury: Inside the Trump Whitehouse," by Michael Wolfe, is an account of the early days of the Trump term. The author was given access to Trump and his aids and is more than negative in his comments.

We can be quite sure that few, if any, pro-Trumpers have read any of these. They would have been devastated by the evidence if they believed. But they believed only what had heard from The Donald, Rush, or Hannity. You certainly don't want facts or contrary opinions to challenge your identity!

For those Trumpers who could, or would, read, they would have gravitated to "Great Again" by Donald Trump. But reading takes so much time away from shooting practice or video games, that it ranks low on the priorities of many!

LYING AND NEGATIVE PROPAGANDA

We are exposed to so much lying. When you are lying, you might as well go all the way:

➢ A friend of a friend has a cousin in the Pentagon, and she said that Iran's Republican Guards are planning to blow up the White House with an atomic bomb piloted by a drone. So, the President is going to blow up Iran with a pre-emptive atomic strike!

➢ The CIA says that Saddham Hussein has weapons of mass destruction, so we will attack him.

➢ Everybody knows that the Democrats faked 10 million votes in the 2020 election. Trump actually won it.

➢ Q prophesied a great insurrection on Inauguration Day.

➢ The "deep state" was controlling the FDA and was not allowing a vaccine for COVID-19 to be developed quickly. This benefitted Biden's election.

➢ A high-ranking intelligence official, with the *nom de plume* of "Q Clearance Patriot," has revealed that Obama and the "deep state" have interfered with Trump's objectives, like building the wall, stopping the pandemic, and fostering the fake news from CNN, NBC and Bloomberg.

Or they may use non-traditional definitions to validate an identity they have adopted.

➢ Life starts at conception. But there are alternative definitions. The Bible says it is at birth—as do most international laws. Some physicians will say it is when the fetus can live outside the body. Federal law says it is at implantation. A recently produced play had a line that "a Jewish fetus is not viable until it graduates from med school."

➢ Black lives matter—all lives matter. What about Hitler's?

➢ America is racist. While too often true—it has had a black president and vice-president in the last five years—and two Black Secretaries of State in the last 20 years.

It is easy to convince people of the value of their identities and how others are responsible for any wrongs that befall them. During the First World War, the German citizenry was not told that their country was losing. It was puzzling for many that they lost. A few years later, it was Hitler who told them how great their identity was and how the earlier war was lost because of the Social Democratic Party and the Jews.

The Jews have been very busy people. The Christians blamed them for causing the Black Death. An Egyptian governor blamed shark-sightings at an Egyptian resort on Israeli operated remote-controlled sharks. Hitler blamed modern art on a Jewish attempt to control German minds. Oh! And the Jews killed Jesus. Of course they seem to forget, if they ever knew, that Jesus was always a Jew. And oh!, there are so many more equally creditable claims!

We see the acceptance of somewhat questionable evidence by many people who have identities that are often based on outright lies. In the 2016 American election, developers of conspiracy theories started the rumor that high Democratic officials, including Hillary Clinton, were operating a sex trafficking ring from the basement of a pizza parlor in Washington DC. The story was completely false. The pizza parlor did not even have a basement. The far-right propagandists (See Volume I, Chapter 33) spread the rumor to every far-right media channel and Twitter. A man from North Carolina drove up to Washington and fired several shots into the restaurant. He was later found guilty of several charges and was required to pay $5000 in damages to the restaurant owner and was sentenced to four years in prison. The story then prompted people to destroy other pizza restaurants as far away as Texas. Innocent restaurant owners lost customers. Employees lost jobs. Entertainers lost their jobs. Many received death threats.

President Trump said that COVID-19 was just like any other flu. There was no need to wear masks to prevent you from transferring it or getting it. Social distancing is for sissies and Democrats. The fact that the U.S. had over 24 million cases and over a quarter million deaths within eight months of his statement, and things got worse from there. It didn't alter his opinion. And, that opinion was contrary to the facts being followed by about every other country. Even though he contracted the disease and was eventually vaccinated, the faithful identities followed blindly his earlier pronouncements.

This is exactly the type of fake news that the Russians, Chinese, and Iranians use to disrupt elections in the West. But it is more dangerous when the far-right propagandists use it—and they can, because of the Supreme Court's definitions of freedom of speech that allow speech, no matter how untrue, to be legal. This is because, as previously mentioned, that the First Amendment clearly specifies that, "Congress shall make **NO** law abridging the freedom of speech or of the press." And while Amendments 9 and 10 give to the states, or the people, rights not prohibited by the Constitution, the Supreme Court has determined that states may make no laws that interfere with the near absolute right of saying, or writing, whatever one will—as long as it doesn't provoke violence in the next 5 or 10 minutes, or object to a declared war or military action taken by the United States. You might think that objecting to a war would be absolutely protected by an absolute right to free speech—but NO! You are allowed to promote violence in the society (Brandenberg v Ohio) but not to protest against international violence (Schenck v. U.S.)

One might think that the states and the people would have rights that other amendments give them, such as:

Article 9... The enumeration in the Constitution, of certain rights, shall not be construed to deny or disparage others retained by the people.

Article 10... The powers not delegated to the United States by the Constitution, nor prohibited by it to the States, are reserved to the States respectively, or to the people.

So the Supreme Court has ruled, that if Congress is prohibited from doing something, so are the states!

FAKE NEWS

Donald Trump was calling all legitimate investigative journalism as "fake news" because it disagreed with what he wanted the people to believe, but he embraced the real fake news of the oil and coal companies that wanted people to believe that either there was no change in the climate, or if there were--that fossil fuels were in no way to blame.

Tobacco companies had used the same type of lies years before. So the Constitution, as interpreted by the Supreme Court, aids in concealing the truth from Americans.

Intelligent people can disagree on basic assumptions. They can disagree on whether liberty or equality are more important to an ideal society. They can disagree on just how much equality of opportunity should be allowed. But intelligent people will not argue against empirically verifiable evidence.

- The world is not flat.
- The planet is warming.
- Legal and illegal drugs do more harm than good for a society.
- For an optimally functioning society--freedom must be responsibly used.

Can you trust the government? The BBC of the UK? Yes. RT from Russia? No. When the government controls the press, you can expect propaganda that supports the leader's view. The more autocratic the leader, even if democratically elected, the more he wants the press controlled. "He" is used here because female leaders seem to be more concerned with their societies than their personal power. This may be why female-led countries are considerably happier, more democratic, and less corrupt. They also are adept at avoiding war--the sissies!

So fake news is all around us. How do we sort the wheat from the chaff, the lies, from the half-truths, from the rationalizations--and find the objective truth?

COMPETING VALUES--EVALUATING THE EVIDENCE

Let's assume that my friend and I want very much to spend the afternoon with each other. I want to go to a movie but he wants to play tennis. How do we resolve the problem? We can flip a coin. We can do like I want this week and what he wants next week. We could let a third-party choose for us. Or we could seek additional evidence.

What if the movie is a comedy, we laugh and are relaxed, but that is all? What if the movie is a documentary about police brutality, which excites us to join a Black Lives Matter protest? But then we are arrested or shot. What if the film is an historical portrayal that excites me to study history in college?

The film costs money, and playing tennis at the public court does not. Is cost a factor?

But what if we choose tennis? We will be better conditioned after playing. But what if I sprain my ankle, get hit in the eye with the ball, or develop a tennis elbow?

We need more information before we embark on our chosen activity. What is the subject of the movie? What are the chances that I will sprain my ankle playing tennis?

Whenever we have competing values, or even a single value, if we are intelligent, we look at possible positives and negatives to a value or an action.

HOW DO WE MAKE THE COUNTRY MORE INTELLIGENT IN CHOOSING VALUES AND EVIDENCE?

It is obvious that the way the Supreme Court has interpreted the First Amendment allows falsehoods that can destroy the republic. A new amendment is needed to bring that First Amendment in line with the Preamble's phrase "to promote the general welfare."

Improving education is an obvious necessity. This requires several factors:

1. Constitutional changes
2. More highly educated teachers
3. A national non-partisan civics, political science, and logic curriculum.

4. We might consider a proficiency test, for elected and appointed officials on: history, economics, logic, biology and environmental science. If drivers, barbers and brain surgeons need licenses, why not legislators, executives, and judges?

THE CONSTITUTION AND FREE SPEECH--DO COURT DECISIONS FIT YOUR IDENTITY?

A Constitutional change to the free speech and freedom of the press guarantees in the First Amendment might be necessary to correct for the dangers to democracies from politicians to be able to lie at will, and for false information to be protected as free speech when it is often the only source of information that some voters have heard. Allowing totally false statements or stories was not the intent of the First Amendment when it was written. Nor was allowing virtual child pornography (Ashcroft v. Free Speech Coalition, 535 U.S. 234 [2002]) or inciting violence with hate speech (Brandenburg v. Ohio, 395 U.S. 444 [1969])

If justice is to be the imperial standard for a society—is it "just" to lie, to fabricate absurdities and disseminate them to the world as if they are truth?

Some legislators and judges don't seem to realize that the realities of 1787, when the Constitution was signed, are not the realities of today. Can we imagine:

➢General George Washington's air force could not reach London to bomb King George.

➢Thomas Jefferson's word processing program occasionally didn't work because the Monticello electrical grid often malfunctioned.

➢James Madison's Facebook page was below par in uploading the photos of his dog!

But those men, our Founding Fathers, were educated, far-thinking statesmen well aware of the weaknesses and lack of education of the public. Historians opine that our founders would be aghast at the lies and absurdities that are published and believed by so many citizens—and that these falsehoods are protected by the Constitution that they wrote.

At the time that the Constitution was written, the average literacy rate of the European-Americans was about 70%. Indians and slaves were generally illiterate. The Founding Fathers were both highly literate and intelligent.

James Madison, in 1799, wrote, "In every State, probably, in the Union, the press has exerted a freedom in canvassing the merits and measures of public men of every description which has not been confined to the strict limits of the common law." It was expected that the press would be honest— even while advocating different values.

THE GUARANTEES OF THE PREAMBLE

It is obvious that the writers of the Constitution believed that the Preamble was an essential element of the Constitution. Alexander Hamilton wrote in Essay 84 of the Federalist (The Federalist Papers), that he didn't see a need for a Bill of Rights because the rights needed are all covered in the Preamble.

"Here, in strictness, the people surrender nothing, and as they retain every thing, they have no need of particular reservations. 'We the people of the United States, to secure the blessings of liberty to ourselves and our posterity, do ordain and establish this constitution for the United States of America.' Here is a better recognition of popular rights than volumes of those aphorisms which make the principal figure in several of our state bills of rights, and which would sound much better in a treatise of ethics than in a constitution of government.

"On the subject of the liberty of the press, as much has been said, I cannot forbear adding a remark or two: In the first place, I observe that there is not a syllable concerning it in the constitution

of this state, and in the next, I contend that whatever has been said about it in that of any other state, amounts to nothing. What signifies a declaration that 'the liberty of the press shall be inviolably preserved?' What is the liberty of the press? Who can give it any definition which would not leave the utmost latitude for evasion? I hold it to be impracticable; and from this, I infer, that its security, whatever fine declarations may be inserted in any constitution respecting it, must altogether depend on public opinion, and on the general spirit of the people and of the government. And here, after all, as intimated upon another occasion, must we seek for the only solid basis of all our rights.

But the Supreme Court, being far wiser than Hamilton, has taken an opposite view. The Preamble has meaning only when it suits them. Absolute liberty may be constrained when it comes to having an abortion or to non-believers being required to support church activities with their taxes when the churches are not taxed. But it has given to the press the duty of exposing politicians when they lie!

In Jacobson v. Massachusetts, (197 U.S. 11 [1905]), the plaintiff refused to be vaccinated, as required by state law, based on his right to liberty as found in the Preamble of the Constitution. The Supreme Court held that the only legal liberties are spelled out in the Articles that followed the Preamble.

"We pass without extended discussion the suggestion that the particular section of the statute of Massachusetts now in question (§ 137, chap. 75) is in derogation of rights secured by the preamble of the Constitution of the United States. <u>Although that preamble indicates the general purposes for which the people ordained and established the Constitution, it has never been regarded as the source of any substantive power conferred on the government of the United States, or on any of its departments</u>. Such powers embrace only those expressly granted in the body of the Constitution, and such as may be implied from those so granted. Although, therefore, one of the declared objects of the Constitution was to secure the blessings of liberty to all under the sovereign jurisdiction and authority of the United States, no power can be exerted to that end by the United States, unless, apart from the preamble, it be found in some express delegation of power, or in some power to be properly implied therefrom. 1 Story, Const. § 462.

We also pass without discussion the suggestion that the above section of the statute is opposed to the spirit of the Constitution. Undoubtedly, as observed by Chief Justice Marshall, in 1819, speaking for the court in *Sturges* v. *Crowninshield*, 4 Wheat. 122, 202, 4 L. ed. 529, 550, **'the spirit of an instrument, especially of a constitution, is to be respected not less than its letter; yet the spirit is to be collected chiefly from its words.**' We have no need in this case to go beyond the plain, obvious meaning of the words in those provisions of the Constitution which, it is contended, must control our decision." (Emphasis added.)

Then there is the full Preamble, that Hamilton abbreviated:

"We the People of the United States, in Order to form a more perfect Union<u>, establish Justice, insure domestic Tranquility,</u> provide for the common defence, <u>promote the general Welfare</u>, and secure the Blessings of Liberty to ourselves and our Posterity, do ordain and establish this Constitution for the United States of America."

A preamble can have at least three functions—

    ➢   to be a controlling guide for what follows,

    ➢   to have a limited function for clarifying what follows,

➢to merely introduce what follows without having any legal effect.

Hamilton believed it to be the first option, the Supreme Court has opted for the first option with Marshall's opinion in the Sturges, then the third option in Jacobson--90 years later. And, who might know better? Hamilton was not only present at the convention and a major illuminator of its body and spirit in The Federalist, he was a gadfly in getting the Constitution ratified. So, whose interpretation is most meaningful? Was Marshall's analysis more important? The Jacobson Court mentioned Marshall's opinion, but went on to ignore it.

OUR IDENTITIES AND OUR VALUES

So we start with an identity, or several identities, then accept the evidence that validates that identity. This may, then, change our behavior. If information or propaganda goes against our values, we may disparage the other party, pick up guns to fight the alleged perpetrator, tell our friends, or do any number of things based on the false information.

Dictators commonly take over the free press. And, today, they may call it fake news in order to reduce the impact of the unbiased, or slightly biased, news that may be available to us. How well do you evaluate the evidence you use to validate your values?

DONALD TRUMP CREATED IDENITIES IN MANY PEOPLE

I was amazed at the intelligent people who believed Donald Trump's unsubstantiated charges about Hillary Clinton's emails, in the 2016 election. There was no evidence that there was anything illegal, and subsequent FBI investigations showed that there was nothing. But Donald Trump's continual bombardment with lies, reduced people's trust in her to under 40%. As First Lady, Senator and Secretary of State, she had ratings as high as the 70% range.

The truism is that when you have heard something 20 times or more you will usually believe it. Trump's baseless charges that her emails were illegal, she was corrupt, and that she was totally responsible for the destruction of the American Embassy in Benghazi—resonated with people, whose values were anti-establishment and whose observations were that Congress needed to be shaken up. This probably included a majority of Americans! It was not difficult to motivate people that wanted things better for themselves. Don't we all!!

On his way through the 2016 primaries, Trump continually belittled his opponents, even when they had similar platforms to his—such as with Jeb Bush.

He was easily able to forge many people's identities psychologically. They could identify with his billionaire and celebrity status. Many identified with his anti-Washington approach. They couldn't disprove his promises for a balanced budget, tax cuts, elimination of the national debt, or more jobs. Many identified with his anti-abortion stance. So identities were formed, and formed strong enough to break up families, in the pro- and anti-Trump camps. And strong enough to break Federal law by storming the Capitol then sitting in federal prisons for several years. Those were strong and committed identities.

No American in recent years, or ever!, has created such strong identities in his followers. It was one thing to follow the path laid out by FDR, or to be swept up in the patriotic capitalism of Reagan--both had higher visions for the nation--even though their visions were almost diametrically opposed. But the Trump identities were built on conspiracy theories, unwarranted suspicions, and hate objects. Did he really believe that there was no global warming and climate change? If so, he was totally misinformed and lacked a basic knowledge ecological science. Did he really not believe that Russia had helped him win the election with the help of Cambridge Analytica and a conservative hedge fund operator? Did he really believe that sovereign nations would acquiesce to his demands as contractors once did to get lucrative building contracts?

But his supposed success in business and on television did not transfer to his national leadership. Running a business and running a nation are as different as flying a paper airplane and piloting a 747! This is why businessmen rate very low as presidents, in terms of effective leadership.

Trump's approach was psychologically effective, but logically inept. But, as we have repeatedly said—the great majority of people are motivated psychologically, not logically. We saw Trump, by accident or design, create enough voters, in enough states, to win.

Some of his charges and promises were that:
- Washington DC is corrupt, so we must "clean the swamp,"
- A successful businessman can do it,
- Then he added evangelicals and Catholics with an anti-abortion pledge,
- Illegal Mexicans are rapists and drug dealers,
- He will build a wall to keep Mexicans out—and Mexico will pay for it,
- Muslims threaten America,
- China is taking American jobs,
- Obama didn't work, he played golf,
- There should be no deficits, and the national debt can be eliminated in 8 years,
- We can make America great again,
- We can have 3.5 to 4% or greater economic growth,
- Companies will take back jobs from China,
- Decrease the trade deficit,
- He would work without a salary,
- The COVID-19 pandemic is nothing to worry about,
- The virus will disappear by summer 2020.

After he was elected, he kept telling everyone how great the economy was, how he had reduced unemployment, and how the stock market had increased. The economy he inherited was already good, but he borrowed $3 trillion to give people and corporations tax breaks to keep it going. Who will pay it back?

But at the end of his tenure, we can see a number of promises that he didn't keep. The GNP averaged a 2.5% increase for his term not the 3.5 to 4% he promised. The expected increase in the trend line didn't happen. The chart below shows a steady increase in the economy since 1975—no matter which party controlled the presidency!

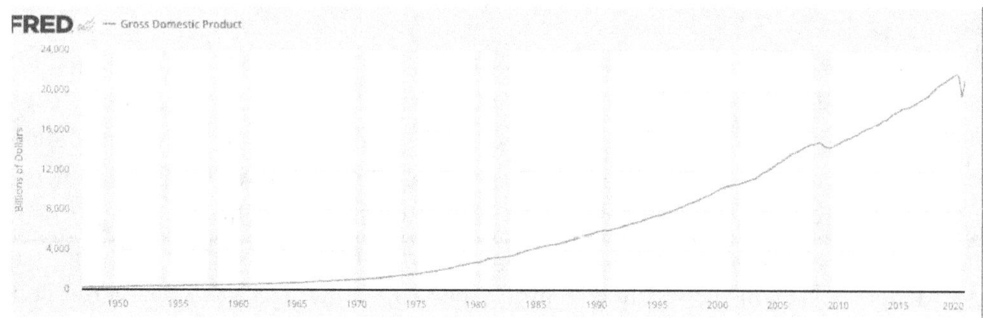

The Trump tax breaks allowed corporations to use more profits for dividends, so the stock market rose. 55% of Americans do own some stocks. The market rose because Trump had reduced corporate and individual taxes. He borrowed $3 trillion to do this. Every trillion borrowed costs every American $3030. Then the interest on every trillion is $60 for every year that it is not paid off. So, if $25 trillion is owed, every American pays between $1150 and $1500 per year as a part of the tax revenue—based on the recent fluctuations in the interest rates. It is near $400 billion annually.

THE FAILURE OF TRUMP'S ECONOMIC PROMISES.

For Trump's years, the economic growth for 2017 was 2.2%, then 3.2% in 2018. It averaged 2.5% from 2017 to 2019, then it dropped in 2020—increasing 2.4% the first quarter. Because of the pandemic, it finished the year down-- dropping 33% the second quarter, then making up 60% of that loss the third quarter. This could only be blamed partially on Trump, because of his denial and mishandling of the pandemic.

The national debt increased from $19.57 trillion in 2016 to more than $27 trillion in 2020. About $3 trillion were because of his tax cuts for corporations and the wealthy.

The trade deficit increased every Trump year. Manufacturing jobs originally increased by 500,000 but by July 2020 there were fewer manufacturing jobs than in 2017. Apple still manufactures in China.

He did increase 200 more coal mining jobs—but thousands more were lost in the pandemic. He did increase steel making jobs by 10.3%.

According to Reuters, Trump's tariffs cost America $46 billion. China's retaliatory tariffs reduced exports to China by $23 billion annually. Forbes estimated the yearly cost of the tariffs to American families was $2031. China just adds the tariff to the wholesale prices it charges, then the American consumer pays the tariff!

Trump's bragging about reducing unemployment is true, but somewhat overstated. The Bush recession, caused by his wars and tax reductions, increased the unemployment rate from 5 to 10% in 2010. Obama reduced it to 4.7% by Jan 2017, the graph shows a straight line to March of 2020 with a rate of 3.5% then it shot up to 14.7 in April because the pandemic was not controlled. By October it reduced to 6.7%.

In the graphs below, we can see that Trump merely continued the trend line of Obama. Both used massive borrowing, Obama to restart the recession he inherited from Bush, and Trump to keep the good economy growing and to give massive tax breaks for corporations and billionaires. Luckily, he benefitted on both counts.

The chart below, from the Bureau of Labor Statistics shows employment, rather than unemployment numbers.

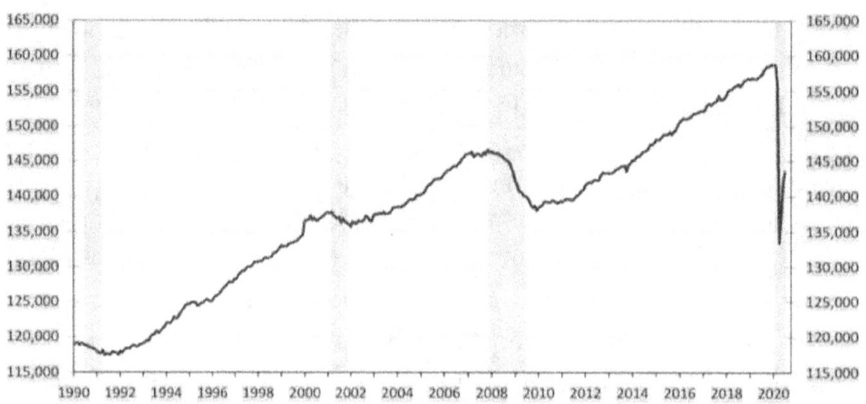

Another way to look at employment is by viewing the percent of the population that is actually employed.

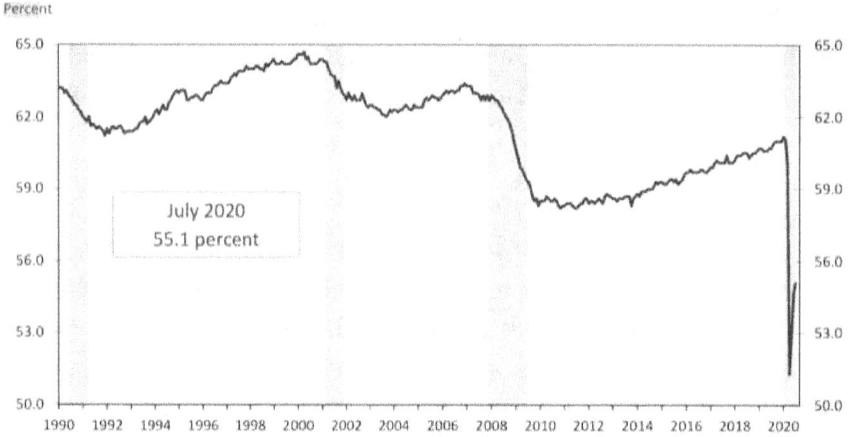

You see that Trump's employment levels did not approach that achieved by Clinton or Bush. Bush created 5.7 million jobs, Obama 8.9 million, and Trump 6.6 million. As mentioned, each used increasing the national debt to increase employment.

Trump kept telling the people how good he had made the economy, and they believed him. All they needed to do was look at the government's statistics.

WHAT ABOUT GOLF?

Then there were his accusations that Obama played too much golf—and that Trump would be working for the people—not playing!

Obama played golf 98 times his first term. Trump played 285 times until the election. Then he played more. Each trip to Mira-Lago cost about a million dollars per trip, about $141,000,000 in total. Of course, he was not taking the $400,000 presidential salary! Golf cart rental charged to the U.S. government has been $760,000 but that is to a private contractor, not Trump. Of course, the contractor pays Trump a yearly fee to provide the carts to golfers. On the other hand, he reportedly charged the Secret Service $650 per room per night.

If you are intelligent, and of course you are--or you wouldn't have read this far!, you have social concerns as part of your identity. Do you want steep tax increase in your payroll or income taxes? How about a cut in your pension? How about working more years to collect that pension? How about paying more for your French wine, Your Japanese TV or your "everything" from China. For the countries with currencies pegged to the dollar it won't affect you much. Your wine from Hong Kong or your computers from Qatar will cost American prices.

Estimate for the national debt in 2030 by the Congressional Budget Office in January of 2020 was $31 trillion. As of July 14, 2021 it was $28 trillion. That is bad--but how bad? We have traditionally used the figure of 77% of a country's GNP as the level of borrowing that is dangerous. Higher than that level, it was found a gradual reduction of the growth of national output.

New International Monetary Fund (IMF) research has backed off the 77% but is not certain of the long-term effects. However, factors such as the country's bond rating, the interest rate that must be paid, the tax revenue, the expenses of the government, the willingness of taxpayers to pay the expenses of the government, and the willingness of the government to allow state ownership of some industries (state capitalism). Here is a government chart, updated daily, that shows the debt as of July 14, 2021. Trillions more were added before the end of the year to update a much-needed national infrastructure overhaul.

Balance Transactions	Closing balance today	Opening balance		
		Today	This month	Fiscal year
Debt Held by the Public	$ 22,290,774	$ 22,289,664	$ 22,329,823	$ 21,018,952
Intragovernmental Holdings	6,170,382	6,187,410	6,199,613	5,926,439
Total Public Debt				
Outstanding	28,461,156	28,477,074	28,529,436	26,945,391
Less: Debt Not				
Subject to Limit:				
Other Debt	478	478	478	478
Unamortized Discount	21,289	21,301	21,376	17,271
Federal Financing Bank	6,053	6,053	6,053	7,262
Hope Bonds	0	0	0	0
Plus: Other Debt Subject to Limit				
Guaranteed Debt of				
Government Agencies	0	0	0	0
Total Public Debt				
Subject to Limit	$ 28,433,335	$ 28,449,242	$ 28,501,528	$ 26,920,380

The Trump proposal, in his 2021 proposed budget, estimated that in 2030 the budget deficit, and therefore the yearly increase in national debt, will be $775 billion—about $2350 more debt per person and $2300 to $3100 per person annual interest (assuming both 2% and 3% interest rates)! The interest rate on current borrowing varies from 0 to 2%. But what if the interest rises to the level of 30 years ago? We would each owe five to ten times as much!

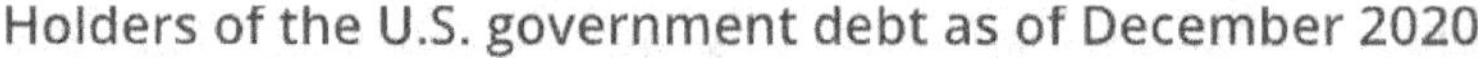

Holders of the U.S. government debt as of December 2020

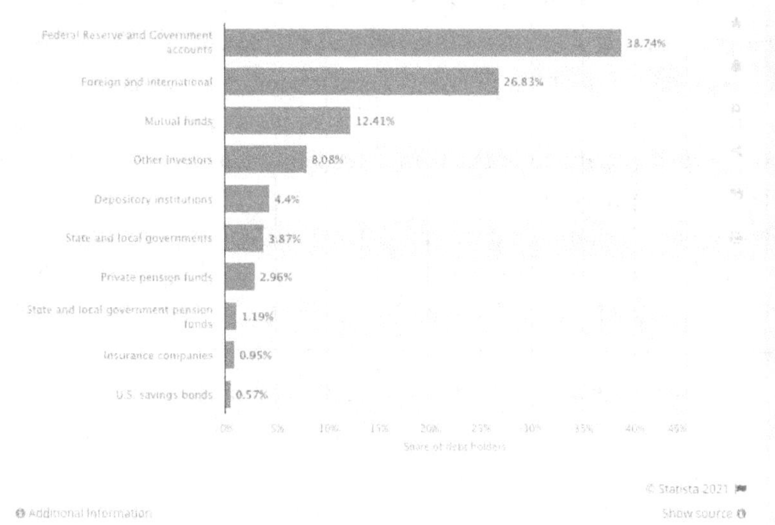

Add these numbers to the average person's share of their state's debt of $3,600 and the average personal debt of $63,000 and you owe a lot of money. Of course, we don't see much of this debt except for monthly house payments and credit card bills. Politicians keep our national debt hidden!

Is your identity measured only by the size of your bank account today, or is it concerned with the future of the country and the financial well-being of your grandchildren? Are you concerned that your Social Security retirement check will be too little to live on? Are you concerned that thar post-retirement European tour will be financially out of reach? A well thought out identity considers both the past and the future.

THE PRO-TRUMP IDENTITIES

Two acquaintances of my daughter are pro-Trumpers because of his tax breaks. Both are successful small businessmen--one is a 300e remodeling contractor, the other is a recruiter for engineers. Both are high school graduates of above average intelligence, but lacking in a knowledge of economics. In a discussion with them, they were insistent that the government just printed money and that the money would not affect the present or future value of the dollar. The international economic facts, such as international borrowing, the devaluing of the dollar, the reduction of America's borrowing ability, and the higher national interest rates of borrowing with increased inflation, did not "compute" with them. It reminded me of what the title character on the early TV sit-com, "Life of Riley," would say when challenged because of an ignorant decision he was making, "My head's made up!"

Tax cuts may be needed in recessions to stimulate the economy, but the "trickle down" propaganda of Reagan, Bush and Trump, while it may get votes, doesn't work as promised-- and the rich just get richer.

TAXES AND THE NATIONAL DEBT--DO YOU CARE?

As was illustrated in Volume One, too many people are too uninformed, selfish, or stupid to either know about the national debt or to care about its ramifications. Here is an illustration from a recent year, 2019, when we owed less than $23 trillion. Our leaders had borrowed almost $17 trillion from other governments and investors, and $6 trillion from our own retirement funds and Medicare. So now the government is on the hook for paying the continually increasing medical costs and the many government pensions. You can see that the government borrowed $3 trillion from the Social Security Trust fund. Do you trust them with your funds?

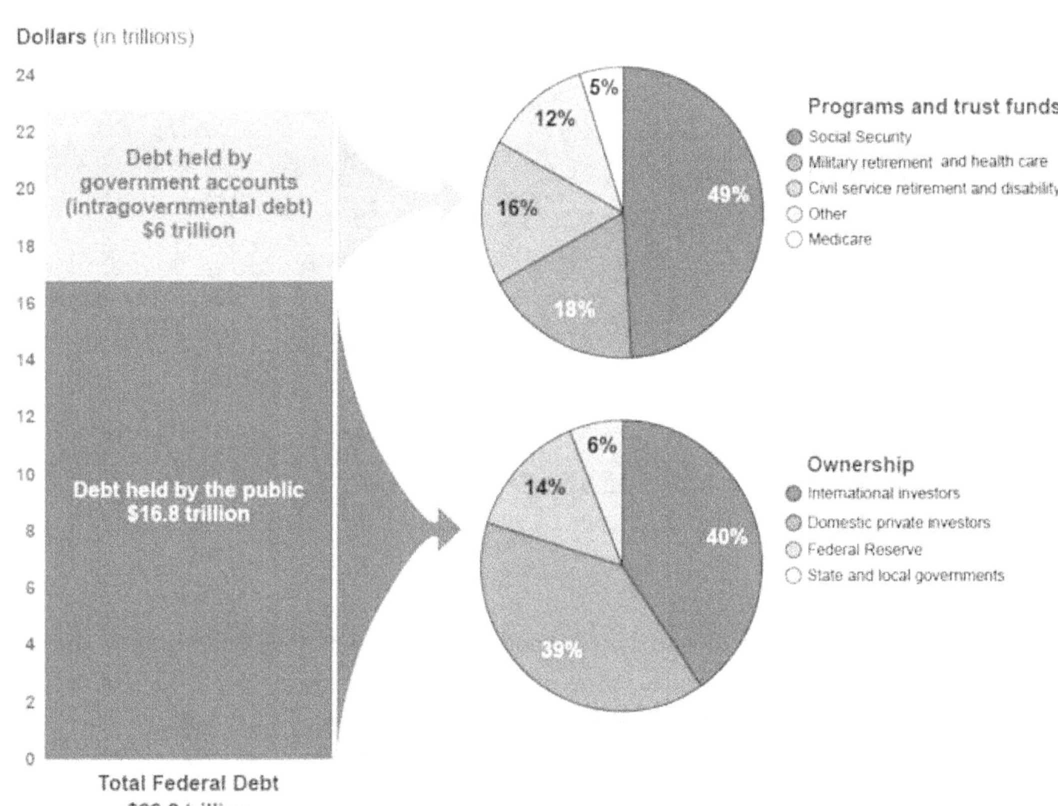

In the last two years, to March 2021, the debt has increased to $28.1 trillion. A number of other countries have lent us money. Japan $1.28 trillion, China $1.06 trillion, Switzerland, Ireland, Brazil, Luxembourg and the UK each own from $250 to $450 billion. Then there are other countries and foreign investors that own a total of $3.2 trillion. So, we owe outsiders a bit over $7 trillion, or about 25% of what we have borrowed.

That other 75% is largely borrowed from your retirement funds: federal, state and private. Your government borrowed nearly $5 trillion from your Social Security fund, the Military Retirement Fund and other Federal retirement funds. It has borrowed over a trillion dollars from states and municipalities, largely pension funds. It has borrowed over $784 billion from private pension funds and a quarter of a trillion from insurance companies, much of that should fund pensions or health insurance. Then it has borrowed a third of a trillion from Medicare contributions. Mutual funds and other American investors hold another $6 trillion.

Oh! We pay interest on that debt from our tax revenue. The interest is about $280 billion on our external debt and $120 billion on that borrowed from our pension funds and Medicare. The government now pays only about a 2.2% as its interest rate. In 2020 it was 2%, in 2030 it is projected to be 3.2%. So, if we don't borrow any more money, we will be paying about $430 billion. But if the federal interest rate rises to over 6.5%, as it did in the late 1990s, we would be paying about $1.2 trillion in interest. That would be about 63% of total amount of personal income taxes collected this year. The Office of Budget Management offers this overview of where the government revenues are sourced.

This where we get the money to run the government (in billions of dollars.

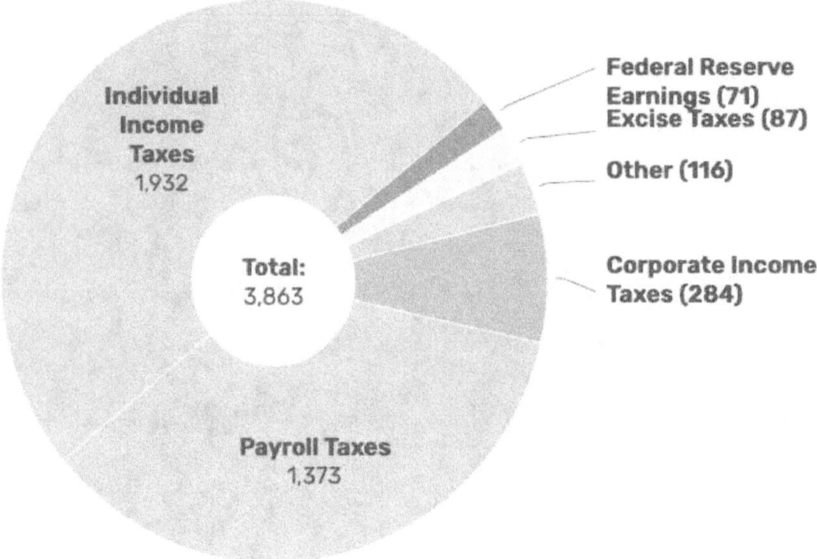

But Biden would like to borrow another $7 trillion for infrastructure and other spending. It is highly doubtful that he would get so much. But for Americans is necessary infrastructure, like roads, bridges, and 5G internet as important as tax breaks?

We already know that every party, major and minor, wants to rule. And in America how do they become elected? By promising more goodies for you and letting other taxpayers pay for it. Trump promised tax relief for all--more for the rich guys and corporations. Biden promised to tax only those making more than $400,000 a year. Will the $400,000+ people still continue to contribute to Democratic candidates? Of course, unless that tax codes are changed. But which party wants to do that?

The American government is working a Ponzi scheme that, if it was a private citizen would land it in jail. Ponzi schemes give the initial investors big profits. Our government has given more money to all through tax reductions. Corporations and the rich benefit the most. But all are happy. In a Ponzi scheme the people who make the money tell others how good it is. So, people vote for those who will give them more tax breaks. But as in Ponzi schemes, while the people on top made money, eventually there is not enough to pay everyone--and the scheme collapses. Then the perpetrators went to prison. But are legislators still live lavishly!

As examined in the first volume, American federal taxes are unfair. 25 of the richest Americans paid little to no federal income tax in recent years, and did it legally. Amazon's Jeff Bezos' wealth increased by $127 billion, according to Forbes, but he reported a total of $6.5 billion in income, and paid $1.4 billion in personal federal taxes is a massive number — yet it amounts to a 1.1% true tax rate on the rise in his fortune." Elon Musk, the world's second richest man, and Carl Icahn, the 40th wealthiest America, paid no personal income taxes--legally. The average tax rate in the U.S. is 14.6%. And over 40% of Americans pay no personal income taxes.

Warren Buffet paid slightly under $24 million in taxes from 2014 to 2018 on a reported earnings of $125 million. Yet, his wealth increased by $24.3 billion. So his true tax rate was about 0.10%. Buffet is noted for telling all that the Tax Code is unfair to us peons. He reminds us that his secretary pays a higher tax rate on her earnings than he does. Of course, he is a great philanthropist--believing that he would rather help people today than fund the reduction of our mismanaged budget and our national debt.

As illustrated in the first volume, our Tax Code could use some reworking--or better, a total overhaul! We should consider how people accumulate income. Should there be different tax rates for people who earned their money by working with one's hands or brain, investing, or inheriting. In our capitalistic system we have encouraged people to make money. Consequently, expenses such as for research or for interest payments are exempt from taxes. Investment income from the sale of property or stocks is taxed at a much lower rate. Inheritance taxes are incredibly low.

WHAT ABOUT IDENTITIES?

At least a part of an intelligent person's identity will be related to one's society, the effectiveness of the government, and the future direction of the country. For people who believe how they are governed is important, how can their identities be stimulated to foster changes for the good? What are their society-based value assumptions? Or, do they have any? If you do, how can they best be exemplified? Might you:

▪ Support candidates that you think will run the school board, city, state or nation the way you perceive to be the best--after you have done an extensive survey of ideas, ideals, and facts.

▪ Run for a government position yourself?

▪ If you are a lawyer, accountant, or economist, you might write academic or popular articles about how the government should work.

▪ You might join groups that support causes you hold dear, such as: Greenpeace, Planned Parenthood, or a political party or action group.

Your identity will change as you adopt different values. Do you think that Alexandria Ocasio-Cortez has a different view of herself as an elected and vocal member of the House of Representatives than she did as a student or a bartender? How about Anthony Gonzales moving from pro football into the House?

If you think some major changes need to be made to the Constitution, like:

➢a balanced budget requirement

➢the way the Supreme Court is chosen

➢whether the Preamble should be as important as the words that follow it in Supreme Court decisions

➢whether there should be a mandatory pay-down of the national debt

➢	whether for efficiency and achievement the education systems and healthcare systems should be nationalized

➢	whether capital punishment should be mandated or made illegal, whether gerrymandering should be illegal

➢	whether voting rights should be controlled by the national government

➢	whether potential parents would have to pass a test on parenting before conceiving

➢	whether abortion should be legal

➢	whether the make-up of the Senate should be changed.

There are so many options. But some, like changing the Senate's make-up has no chance because there is no way to have the states with smaller populations to vote to reduce their legislative impact.

There are 29 states, of the 34 necessary, ready to call a Constitutional Convention. A balanced budget amendment is one of the issues that might be considered. Most U.S. states, along with nations such as: Germany, Hong Kong, Italy, Poland, Slovenia, Spain and Switzerland, are among the countries that already have balanced budget requirements.

TO REINFORCE OUR IDENTITIES, WE PURSUE ANY IDEA THAT VALIDATES THEM!

There is always someone who will tell you what you want to hear: priests, politicians, Russian trolls, tabloids, partisan political commentators, neighbors or social media. Do you want to believe in voodoo, human sacrifice, Martians, buried treasure, a happy hereafter, your political party, anti-vaccinations, the necessity of eating hallucinogenic mushrooms or smoking dope, or any of the many thousands of ideas that are floating around that may perch in your brain. And, will you look for evidence that will validate your vision.

In April of 2021 the administrator of a Florida private school announced that she would not hire any teachers who had been vaccinated against COVID. She said that "tens of thousands of women all over the world" have reported reproductive issues from being in close proximity with someone who has been vaccinated — a claim that top medical experts have debunked. Such a policy was dangerous to students and teachers. Why would such a dangerous and false policy be announced? The most likely answer is that the administrator was highly influenced by Trump's early policies. But Trump had been vaccinated, after having the disease. Whether she had developed the policy because of an identity that was based on overcoming a rather severe inferiority complex or based on an anti-Democratic identity is not known. But it is another example of fueling one's identity with evidence that is false and dangerous.

As a therapist, I have worked with people with multiple personalities and others who had invisible helpers flying around the house. I found it rather difficult to believe, but there were books certifying the existence of the invisible creatures. And for one multiple personality, the woman alternated between being a prostitute, a housewife and Elijah. We all know that prostitutes exist, and Elijah is mentioned in the Bible, and she was a verifiable housewife. So in her neurosis, she certainly had evidence!

But now, lets look at how we may evaluate evidence.

SECTION III LOGIC-- AND LIVING AS RATIONAL HUMANS

As we have observed several times, most behavior is elicited psychologically, not logically. Still, our more valuable ideas are those that are more probable due to their empirical validity and reliability. There is no question that ideas, in general, and political exhortations, in particular, should be evaluated by the tools of inductive logic, then our behavior and the promises of politicians should be analyzed by the rules of deductive logic to determine whether they hang together and should be believed.

The evaluations of the current status of our beliefs, and the worthiness of the values we follow, can be clarified, criticized and assessed by cerebral tools superior to our feelings.

Opinions, rather than objective provable truth, have always been the standards for humanity. Myths are easier to believe than quantum physics, or the mysteries of the telescope or the microscope. The world was created in seven days—in 4004 BC, on the 23rd of October, according the Irish Anglican bishop James Ussher. Astronomers, measuring the speed at which the universe is expanding, date the Big Bang at about 13.8 billion years ago. Who should we believe? Maybe, as fervent democrats, we should compromise at 7 billion BCE!

If opinion doesn't determine truth, why should we listen to the pundits of propaganda. They make such strong cases for issues—if we are not concerned with facts! But facts are so often uncomfortable for our identities! And, our fragile identities are rooted in our often well-meaning but ineffective parents and our inferior educations. But politicians are powerless to improve parenting and are afraid of effective educations—how many of today's legislators would have been elected by informed voters?

Our last century has clearly shown, in both wars and protests, an incomplete understanding of the facts and the lack of a logical projection of the evangelized disinformation. How many Germans in 1945 would again vote for Adolf? How many of the invaders of the Capitol in January of 2021, sitting in their federal prison cells, would again follow The Donald?

Values, such as ethics, to be creditable, must be correctly informed and logical.

CHAPTER 6 THINKING EFFECTIVELY BY ANALYING THE EVIDENCE

HOW DO WE KNOW WHAT WE THINK WE KNOW?

Well we've looked a bit at basic assumptions that are always fundamental to our thinking. They are not as simple as they might appear on the surface. A god-based assumption might be theistic, polytheistic, pantheistic or a number of other possibilities. A society-based assumption might include various economic possibilities of a society, political possibilities, problems of liberty versus equality, or civil rights versus the safety of the population. So each basic assumption will vary with the individual 'assumer.' Two Muslims may very well disagree on their basic assumptions, just as two Christians might. So what we are assuming can vary greatly, even if we think that we are assuming the same assumption.

We often mistake our feelings and opinions for thinking. We have an identity (Black, Catholic, Muslim, Sunni, Shia, Democrat, Republican, gym member, business owner, bird watcher, astrologer, vegetarian, Green Peace member, PETA member, atheist, creationist, neighborhood residency, university or high school alum—you get the picture!). Commonly, we look for evidence to back up the position that is implicit in our identity. What if the evidence was clear that one of the bits of evidence you use to validate your identity was totally wrong on an issue?

> What if there really was climate change and that the dangers were severe, but your political party denied that it was true?

> What if there is a conflict between the fact that climate change is caused by too many people in the world using polluting substances with your religion's or government's advocacy of having more children?

> What if your university is dropping rapidly in the world's academic ranking of universities?

> What if the evidence of science clearly proved that the universe began quite differently than your scriptures described, or that evolution, rather than an instant creation of animal and humans had occurred.

Could you, or would you, adjust your identity and beliefs to the proven realities of science? If a more plausible theory for one of your beliefs was developed, would you thoroughly analyze it, or just dismiss it because it because it doesn't fit with your identity?

But before we begin to do what we call "thinking," we must look at the evidence available to us that will build on our basic assumptions. The better the evidence we use, the better the chance we have of leading an intelligent and fulfilling life. And the evidence we use will vary even more than will our basic assumptions.

Any basic assumption can be the ladder up to happiness, or down to despair-- depending on the truth of the evidence we use and its applicability to our assumptions and to our lives. But some evidence is better than others. We can look at empirical evidence, evidence that is provable over and over again. Then there's historical evidence that happened once and that may or not have been eye-witnessed. Of course our traditions, both religious and secular, are extremely important and controlling in our lives—even if they may actually be harmful to our functioning. Then there are the ideas that come from religious or secular authority. And we shouldn't forget that reasonable ideas are often found in philosophy. We might even count on our common sense—but common sense is actually quire uncommon because, as we said, we generally mistake our feelings for thinking.

 How verifiable is the evidence? This should be our major concern. Is the historical evidence that Socrates or Jesus lived as strong as the evidence that hydrogen and oxygen are the ingredients for water? For over two millennia, Socrates' prison was considered to be on the Pnyx, a hill across from the Acropolis,—now it is considered to be in the agora, on the other side of the Acropolis. How accurate was our historical evidence? Is the evidence presented on the 6 o'clock news in New York as verifiable as that heard on the BBC in London. Is the fact that the electric light generally comes on when you flick the switch as verifiable as the claims of politicians that they have improved the education in your country? Was the flood in New Orleans after Hurricane Katrina as verifiable as the Biblical flood of Noah?

It is essential to understand the verifiability of the knowledge that we use to back up our basic assumptions. The next volume will look at a number of societal and individual concerns from the points of view of each basic assumption and the evidence we may use to validate them.

Thomas Jefferson said "I was bold in the pursuit of knowledge, never fearing to follow truth and reason to whatever results they led." Now, at the University of Virginia, which he founded, scientists have looked for evidence of reincarnation, 'near death' and 'out of body experiences' and other paranormal experiences. It is not uncommon for dying people to experience a bright light and see a loved one or a religious figure such as Jesus, Buddha or Moses, or a person or two dressed in white. The Vatican has confirmed that Pope Pius XII had such an experience and saw Jesus, who told him that his hour for death had not yet come. How verifiable is this para-psychological evidence? Is it really just the brain playing tricks? How many Muslims see Jesus on their death beds? How many Buddhists see Mohammad?

Some scientists have duplicated these out of the body experiences in people using electrical stimulation in certain brain areas.

Another area of the para-normal is telepathy. There is a great deal of evidence that some people can read some people's minds. Many years ago, the studies of Dr. Rhyne at Duke University seemed to have proved this. The Soviets did a great deal of work in this area. But the means by which telepathy is done are unknown. It is probably not like radio waves because experiments have been done that seem to discount that possibility.

I remember a number of years ago when I was president of the Malibou Lakeside Club some people wanted to rent the clubhouse for an event. The group were into spiritual sorts of things and felt they could astral travel. They came to a board meeting and wanted to show their special powers. They asked us each to tell them somebody they should visit. Dr. John Messina our vice president volunteered. John was the head physician at the Motion Picture Hospital in Woodland Hills. He was treating film personality Godfrey Cambridge at the time. So he concentrated on Godfrey and the people flew their minds to the hospital and correctly described Godfrey in the hospital. So then I volunteered.

But I cheated. I gave them the name of one of my friends and told where he lived. But I concentrated on another friend who looked nothing like the first. The magic people described the one I was thinking about, not the one they were supposed to fly to. Their skill was obviously telepathy, not astral traveling. Telepathy is a skill that I would never have, so I was impressed. But when I told them what I had done they were really upset. But they still rented the lodge.

I recently saw a TV program with a spiritualist who said he could communicate with the dead. People in the audience would stand up and he would tell them things about themselves that their dead relative was telling him. They verified what he said. I thought that his skill was more likely to be telepathy—reading the minds of the people standing. Of course they verified what he said. Whether he was reading minds or communicating with dead husbands we'll probably never know. But it made for interesting TV.

If telepathy exists, the evidence for reincarnation, that a person has been born before, may be explained by the possibility that a newborn baby's mind has read the mind of one who is dying or one who has lived at the same time as the newborn? If this is so, the newborn would remember some or all of the memories of the transmitting mind. When a person in India believes she has been reincarnated, neighbors accept it because it is a major belief in the Hindu religion. When it happens in a Judeo-Christian society it is usually passed off as an hallucination because the Judeo-Christian religion holds that we have only one life, then we head up or down at the end of it.

I remember a famous case where an American woman thought she had been an Egyptian princess in a former life. She could even speak some Egyptian. But a researcher working to verify the story found that she spoke modern, not ancient, Egyptian. He also found that an Egyptian family had lived in the same building when she was a child. Was this reincarnation or merely the work of the sub-conscious mind and some imagination?

Does the historical evidence of reincarnation give us hope? Is this because we can't think of our own nonexistence? Or is it that we don't want our existence to end?

Based on our limited view of the whole world, we once thought that the world was flat. Our idea of time was similarly limited. St. Augustine and Isaac Newton saw it as we see it, we just look at the clock. But Einstein saw the speed of light as the ultimate measure of time. Many of our new technologies are based on Einstein's theory of relativity rather than Newtonian, Augustinian or Aristotelian concepts of time—or science. Aristotle wrote that women had fewer teeth than men. He never bothered to count them. He said that heavy objects fall faster than light objects, but never tested his statement for truth. The reason that empirical science is the best way of knowing is that we keep developing better tools of knowledge and when we investigate an idea we keep testing and retesting it.

The tools of science become rapidly better allowing scientists to observe more effectively. For example, the telescope of Galileo, which was only 20-power, was continually improved and eventually replaced by the Hubble space telescope which is 4500 to 8000 power. The two-power microscope of the past gave way to the 1500 power optical scope then to the 500,000 power electron microscope of today.

The measurements for dating changed from memory and stories about the past, to counting tree rings, to carbon 14 dating--for up to 50,000 years, then to radioactivity dating for older remnants of our past.

ARE WE TEACHING OUR STUDENTS TO RECOGNIZE FAKE NEWS?

A 2021 PISA study looked at this measurement. More people are getting their information on screens in recent years (15 year-olds spent 21% of their time watching screens in 2012, but 35% of their time on them in 2018).

Some countries are emphasizing methods of separating truth from falsehoods in schools. They are teaching how to separate subjective from objective sources of information, how to evaluate evidence, and how to search for the most verifiable evidence. These are essential tools of intelligent minds. With so many people putting out false and potentially harmful information on social media, the need to glean the truth is more important than ever.

The solid bar shows how all students did relative to the expected standard. The arrowheads on the right indicate the levels achieved by students in the higher socio-economic levels. The diamonds on the left indicate the average level of students from lower socio-economic backgrounds.

What we know, or think we know, may come from several types of evidence. We will now look at several sources of our beliefs: empirical science, historical evidence, what we hear from various sources of authority, from our personal experience, from our reasoning abilities, and from our varying levels of faith. These are not categories that are totally independent. Our belief systems may quite logically combine them. For example, you might combine the empirical-historical theory of evolution with your minister's authoritarian idea that God created all things.

EMPIRICAL EVIDENCE

Empirical science may start with hypotheses, which the non-scientists might call theories. Then experiments are designed to prove or disprove the hypothesis. When many experiments yield the same results, it is then called a theory. But new evidence later discovered may change the theory. The idea that the earth was flat was supplanted with the theory that the earth was round, then that it was not quite round but rather an oblate spheroid, flatter at the top and bottom.

Physical science is more verifiable than the social and psychological sciences. Physical anthropology gives evidence but without a complete picture. The Leakey's work in the Olduvai Gorge has given us a great deal of evidence about the pre-human Australopithicus, but we don't have evidence of every evolutionary change from some sort of ape to *homo sapiens*. But as newer scientific tools develop we have been able to fill huge gaps in the findings of the anthropologists.

Of course, physics and chemistry are much more verifiable. Astronomy has many aspects that are exactly measurable. Geology has a large number of measurable areas. But when we come to physiology, psychology or sociology we have more and more variables. It is much more objectively verifiable to measure the speed of a falling object in physics or test a chemical reaction in chemistry than it is to determine the causes of violence in a sociological setting. Still in each of these sciences we can understand the variables. The more the number of variables, the more difficult it is to approach certainty.

But people usually believe what fits their fancies rather than what is verifiable. Many Americans don't believe in evolution but believe in a Bible that has hundreds of inconsistencies and is based on some oral tradition of things that might have happened thousands of years before they were written down. Admittedly there are some gaps in the millions of changes in life forms during the last four million years. But the sciences of geology, biology and chemistry all point strongly in the direction of evolution. But the possible historical recantings in the Bible are not verifiable in any way.

A virgin birth, a worldwide flood, a resurrection, a creation of the world only 6000 years ago. Many have learned these unverifiable ideas at their mothers knee. Most of their friends believe them. Television evangelists tell you they are true. But are they?

In the last 40 years, the number of Americans who believe that God created humans in their present form has dropped 25%, from 44% of the population to 33% of the population. The number who believed that God guided evolution has dropped from 38% of the population to 33%. And, the percentage that believed that God had no part in evolution rose from 9% to 22%.

Below you can see the recent evolution of some religious thinking in America.

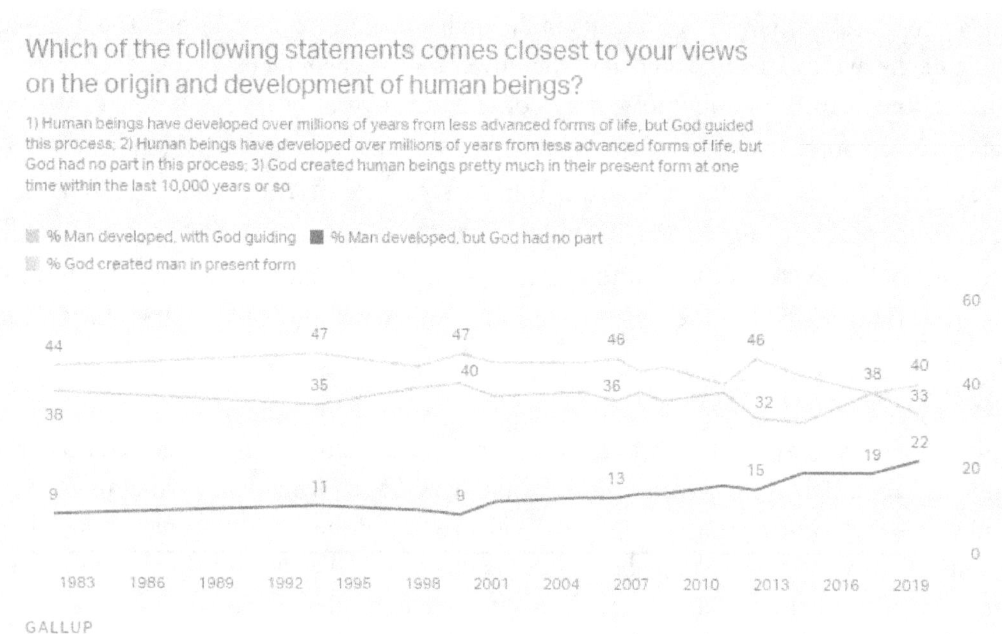

But Americans are not alone in their anti-scientific thinking. The Nazis wouldn't accept Einstein's theories. After all, what could a Jewish pacifist know about the universe? The Soviets wouldn't accept the genetic theories of Mendel or the evolutionary theories of Darwin because they didn't fit the political thinking of the government. So when the Soviet Union wanted to scientifically back up the idea that socially learned abilities could be passed on through the genes they published biologist Lysenko's work as the only science of biology. (His work had been in botany.) It was wrong but it was the only politically acceptable 'science' so everybody had to use it. It put Soviet biologists many years behind because what was called empirical science by the politicians was not true science, and was certainly not verifiable.

We have found the same thing happening recently. With the substantial evidence for global warming known by the scientific community and the general public, the American president George W. Bush, an oil man, first disagreed with its existence, then assigned lawyers to rewrite the scientific reports to obscure the findings of the reputable scientists. Trump did the same thing. The interests of politicians must not be allowed to hold back the advance of science. We might have expected it a hundred years ago in the totalitarian Leninist time, but it should not be possible in a modern educated society. Maybe this is a reason to demand scientifically educated people as our leaders.

But we keep electing lawyers and some businessmen to the high offices. They haven't been educated in the hard sciences. They have usually studied political science, and maybe some history or philosophy, and of course law. Is it too much to ask that they have some knowledge of the problems they are attempting to solve? But how can they be expected to know about climatology, biochemistry, astrophysics, psychology and sociology? It is enough to be told how to vote by the national Democratic and Republican committees!

We all want certainty, but science gives us only probability and the tools to evaluate the probable—looking for the better, not the absolutely certain, explanations. I guess we just have to follow Einstein's advice—to keep questioning.

Science deals with facts, we humans generally deal in emotions, so the facts of science that confront our emotional needs are seldom believed, or are only believed by those with clear unprejudiced minds. Given the tendencies of humans to trust fantasy, it is amazing that science has been allowed to exist. Many fear the unknown, but documented evidence and truth are much scarier!

But our politicians have another psychological force to contend with. If they want to be re-elected, they have to represent their constituencies even if those constituencies are anti-scientific, like the evangelicals or fundamentalist Muslims or Catholics.

World-renowned astrophysicist Stephen Hawking said that the late Pope John Paul II once told him that as scientists they should not study the beginning of the universe because it was the work of God. "It's OK to study the universe and where it began. But we should not inquire into the beginning itself because that was the moment of creation and the work of God." But science is never content to let major questions go unanswered. It must seek answers, verifiable answers. It needs to theorize, then test, then re-test. Empirical science is based on the ideas that when you have a question or problem:

➤First you must define what you mean, determine how to measure it and find out all you can, such as written information.

➤Second, you develop experiments, observations or tests to determine whether a concept or hypothesis is true.

➤Third, you check alternate theories that might explain your findings.

➤You may then retest to check your results.

You may be trying the prove: that the Earth is flat; that there is an unconscious mind; that God exists: that intelligence can be measured; that there was a Trojan War; that Moses existed; that there is a most effective way to make a free throw in basketball; or, that the government is corrupt. There are millions of questions. There are questions about nature, the supernatural, the planets, viruses, evolution, family life, education—and about every large and small aspect of every one of those questions.

Many questions cannot be answered with today's technology. Is there a purple cow on a planet near Alpha Centauri? Is there intelligent life elsewhere in our universe and if so has it contacted us? Some questions cannot be answered because we don't have all the evidence. Was there a Trojan horse? How was Tutankhamen injured? What were the actual missing links between earlier apes and humans? What is the ultimately smallest particle in the universe? How can we find everyone perfect mates—or how do we find anyone a perfect mate?

But as we educate more scientists in more areas and as we increase our technology, better evidence is found and the probability of the truth of our knowledge increases. We find greater probability in certain concepts, such as: the speed of light, the existence of ancient civilizations, the existence of neurotransmitters, how psychoactive drugs work, the theory of evolution.

Hopefully our logical abilities will lead us to a more probable conclusion. But the same evidence does not always lead us to the same conclusion. For example, if we take the three numbers 2, 4 and 8 in a series and ask you to name the next number. You might say 16 or 10, Both would be right, but there are even more possibilities. So the same evidence doesn't necessarily lead to a single conclusion. If you have atoms of hydrogen and atoms or oxygen how might you combine them? Your first thought would be H_2O, water. But they could also form hydrogen peroxide H_2O_2.

Qumran, the site near the where the Dead Sea Scrolls were found was first seen as a monastery of the Jewish sect, the Essenes. Some even thought that Jesus was a member. Many years later a new and more probable theory emerged—that the site was used for pottery making. So as we get more evidence, even in history, our conclusions may change.

Many scientists denied the extensive evidence for global warming. It wasn't until the same evidence was found to be increasing that it became universally accepted by the scientists. Of course it wasn't enough to convince all of the politicians who were protecting their financial links to the businesses that were doing the polluting.

The more intelligent people have no problem admitting that they are wrong. The stupid can never do it. What they think of as their minds—are made up. But a mind made up ceases to exist. A mind must continually question or it isn't working. Evidence and logic have no power to change many people's traditions and customs. But if we do change our beliefs because of the preponderance of the evidence, if we have had the intelligence and conviction to accept beliefs with a higher probability than what we had believed, we risk being called heretics. And only the brave can accept the social disapproval that often comes with using our minds.

STARTING A SCIENTIFIC INQUIRY

In 1905 Albert Einstein published five papers that still excite us with questions about the universe. And. as we discover, as we think and research, the more we know—and, the more we know that we don't know. Some optimists say that we know about 5% of the facts of the universe. That's not bad figuring that empirical science is only a couple of hundred years old. We know little of what we call dark matter which is most of the universe. A hundred years ago we could only hypothesize about atoms, but today we have knowledge of sub-atomic particles, such as photons.

But what good is such research about the universe?

Things like the atomic bomb and the microwave oven have developed because of Einstein's ideas. And now we know that the age of the universe 13 to 14 billion years, and that our galaxy has been around for 11 to 12 billion years, and that our solar system is about 4.5 billion years old. There is no question that such numbers boggle our primitive minds and make us question the myths that were created to explain the unexplainable to our primitive forebears.

HISTORICAL EVIDENCE

Some historical facts are in the realm of science. They are highly verifiable. For some recent happenings, like World War II, we have films and eye witness accounts. But historical evidence is often politicized. Historians can pick and choose what they will examine and report on. Were all German soldiers anti-Semitic? Was Churchill the genius that the British say he was? Did Roosevelt really know that the Japanese were going to attack, but not tell his countrymen? Is history no more than 'a tableau of crimes and misfortunes' as Voltaire maintained? Is it the study of the past, confirming that events never repeat themselves?

Real historians want the truth, although some rewrite history to back up a political or religious system—which often requires ignoring or destroying important documents. We always need to know more about what really happened because so often history is an endless blending of fact and imagination.

Some people deny the evidence because they haven't heard of it. A lack of education, or a lack of objective curricula in one's studies, can leave many people ignorant of many important things that have happened. For example, when the Iranian president Ahmadinejad convened a conference on whether or not the Nazi holocaust of the 1930s and 1940s existed, huge numbers of Muslims had never heard of it. It may not have been because the Muslim world was consciously trying to hide it, although that may have been true. The facts were that millions of Muslims were young and uneducated and what they had heard of genocide in their news reports was about Rwanda and the Balkans in the latter part of the 20th century—particularly about atrocities against Muslims. Additionally, the education of Muslims often includes the idea that Jews are trying to destroy Islam and that they are responsible for AIDS, and for many wars.

Look at the history of Christendom. There are more than thirty known gospels or "glad tidings." Why did the early church fathers in the third century choose only those with the names Matthew, Mark, Luke and John? We know that they were not written by the apostles of the same names. The apostles were probably dead when these gospels were written. The gospel of John was probably written a hundred years after Jesus lived. Why did the early church leaders ignore the gospels of Thomas or Mary or Judas? Were all, some, or none of them actually inspired by God?

There were many sects in area around Palestine at the time of Jesus, such as the Essenes, Nazarenes, Phibionites, Simonites, and others. Why were Jesus's followers so successful? All the sects spoke of the soul going to Heaven, but only Jesus's group talked about the resurrection of the body. This was an idea first proposed by the Zoroastrians. Did the Christians borrow the idea or did it develop independently? There were also other Messiahs at the time of Jesus, but their influence died, while that of Jesus grew. Why?

Religious believers assume the truth of their myths then cite a few historical facts to prove their belief. Yes, a town called Jericho exists. Yes, there is a Temple of Solomon. But what is the proof that the Bible is the inspired word of God? There is no historical proof that Jesus was crucified on Golgotha, that he was resurrected, that he went to heaven. There is only the word of several people writing about it 25 to 100 years after it supposedly happened.

But isn't that how most history has been written? Look at Homer's history of the Trojan wars. Did Agamemnon, Achilles or Hector actually live? Was there ever a Trojan horse? Was Achilles impervious to injuries except for his heel? Was it true that there were gods supporting both sides?

Homer composed his Iliad 500 years after the war. Did he get all of his facts straight? Or was his poem only fantasy? Were any of his ideas changed by the storytellers who recited the epic poem?

We think we can't change the past, but many historians do, especially if they are justifying a cause that is sacred or that backs up their assumptions. From the point of view of the empirical scientist or the serious historian, more proof is needed than the personal experiences of a few people who say they have seen angels, saints, or Jesus.

Religionists say that the chances for a cell developing billions of years ago from inert chemicals are more than a billion to one. That may be true. But the chance of a creator of the universe existing is far greater than that. If probability theory is to be used on one side of an argument, it must be used on the other side as well.

In the area of history, sometimes we have only the words of a single person to indicate an historical event. Sometimes it is an eye witness, such as James Madison telling us about the development of the ideas of the Constitution in the Federalist papers. The 'father of history' Herodotus was not an eye witness to the Peloponnesian Wars. Did he see everything he wrote about? No.

Stonehenge's legends have been many. Some have said the devil bought the stones from a woman in Ireland; another story suggests they were placed on the plain by the fabled wizard Merlin; others have claimed that aliens built the monument and left it as a place for worship, or that Druids built it as a temple for sacrificial ceremonies. Others think that it was first, a place for healing.

The Old Testament, while supposedly happening from the dawn of creation, was not written until a few hundred years before the Christian era (BCE). Of course if it is the inspired word of God, it is certainly correct. Adam and Eve were created about 4000 BCE. Abraham lived about 1800 BCE. Jonah was in the belly of a whale. There was a great flood that covered the earth and wiped out all people and animals in about 2350 BCE. The Red Sea parted for Moses and the fleeing Israelites, then closed in to drown the pursuing Egyptian army in about 1250 BCE. How verifiable is all this?

The New Testament was written closer to the time of Jesus, but probably by people who never knew him. Matthew was probably written by 50 AD, but John probably not until after 100 AD. It is noted that Jesus tends to become more Godlike from Matthew to John. Then Paul, who never met Jesus, becomes his major evangelist. Of course, if it is all the inspired word of God, we can believe it all without analyzing it from the point of view of a critical historian.

Since history is written by the winners we might wonder about the factual situations of the American Revolution. The facts written by the American historians seem to be different from those reported by the English historians of the day.

Getting a bit closer to home, just look at today's textbooks in China. Wars, revolutions, socialism, Marxism and dynasties have been minimized while globalization, economics and technology are now emphasized. Bill Gates, not Chairman Mao, is often a hero. Chinese history is portrayed as much less violent than many of the events of the past might warrant. Modern history points to a more glorious future than to an exalted past.

As so often happens, history in schools and churches leads the students toward the goals that their society desires—toward democracy, socialism, preparation for war, toward economic success, or towards the favored religion. So, history books often use the past to direct students toward a future societal goal, rather than accurately reporting and analyzing events of the past.

It seems that most history is primarily about wars and religion. It seems that quite often societies are actually using the supposed study of history for propaganda for a future society.

History's task has nearly always been to glorify your society's past and aim it at an even more glorious future? But let's get back to history, real history, as evidence. How about eye witnesses to a situation? Judges are quite familiar with eye witnesses to a traffic accident having quite different memories of the same recent event. And it is obviously impossible for a reporter or a group of reporters to remember a whole war, a whole presidential term, or the complete happenings of any historical event. And the farther it is beyond the veils of history, or pre-history, the more mythical it is likely to be.

So, historical evidence is a combination of: "eye witness" accounts, that may not be accurate or complete, tales from people who have heard about it, what the "powers" of religious and secular rulers want us to know, and some people's imaginations. So, unless it is the inspired word of God, as is said to be true of the Bible, the Qur'an, or the Zoroastrian scriptures, we have to place historical evidence at a much lower level of probability than the empirical evidence of physics or chemistry.

But history is not all about oral or written words and traditions. History is often learned or amplified by physical evidence. The Sphinx and the tombs of the pharaohs give us evidence of the Egyptian civilization. The 8,000 terracotta warriors buried in front of the grave of the emperor Qinshihuang's tomb, 2200 years ago, give us a glimpse of ancient Chinese culture—as do the earlier, but less impressive, graves and tombs in China. The foundations of Solomon's Temple and archeological finds in Palestine all give us some physical evidence of history. And the bones and tools of Australopithecus in Tanzania give us some inklings of our distant forbears.

And look at the cave paintings in Australia that date back 28,000 years and in Indonesia—50,000 years. In France and Spain paintings have been found dating from 45,000 to 65,000 years ago. So, the oldest were probably done by Neanderthals. Our species *homo sapiens* probably did not arrive in the area for another 20,000 years. These findings, along with archeological findings, aid us in glimpsing our pre-history.

Is the historical evidence of World War II as verifiable as the evidence of the Peloponnesian wars? Is the evidence that there were once wooly mammoths on the earth as verifiable as the idea that there are elephants on the earth today? Is the evidence that water exists as verifiable as that an oxygen atom has 6 electrons. Is the evidence that the Earth's climate is changing as verifiable as the belief that some people are narcissistic? The physical world offers far more certainty in examining the evidence of chemistry or physics than do the social sciences of sociology or psychology. And how verifiable is the philosophical proposition that the world is matter-- and ideas come from matter, or that the Bible, whose earliest written historical evidence comes from the 2nd Century BC, is accurate in recounting things that happened thousands of years before the physical documents were written?

Certainly, studying our human history is interesting and informative. It may even be able to help us to avoid the mistakes that were made in the past. But it seems that most political and religious leaders ignore the past and attempt to reinvent human progress. But the karma of the deeds of past leaders sweeps leaders of the present into the labyrinth of past errors, and the unlearned lessons of our past imprison the modern heretics who expect human nature to change. Again, the performance of power re-emerges as the tether of past events.

So, while the message of history remains, the players change. The situations change. The rationalizations for the actions of the actors change. It is in the reporting of the actions, actors and oratory--that the evidence of history is questioned. Because nearly every story of our past is obviously charged with the drive for power. And in verifying the psychological drive for power, we can look for the evidence in the science of psychology. So, science is often called upon to verify and illuminate the actions of the people who do the things that historians record and analyze.

Once again, we caution, that--history may be the record of things that never happened, written by people who weren't there.

What we call history is too often propaganda justifying the recent past or the sanctification of ideas our leaders foster and want us to follow—without knowing the real truth. So, ideas or events of history often imprison our minds, rather than set them free.

Here is an example. Muslims are not alone in often being controlled by events of the past. Jihadists have killed Moslems and others in Iraq, Saudi Arabia and Egypt as well as in Southeast Asia. The battle between the reactionary traditionalists and the more rational liberals dates from the 800s in Iraq. But inter-Islamic battles about who should lead the various sects also goes back to the beginnings. Then the Moslem conquests of North Africa, Spain and around the eastern Mediterranean and into southern Asia created more power conflicts about who should lead. The Crusades justifiably fostered an anti-Christian mind set in Muslims. Then more recently the division of Palestine, giving part of it to the Jews, and the American intervention in Iraq and Afghanistan created more hostility.

George W. Bush thought that by conquering Iraq he could instill his ideas of democracy, and that freedom and respect for the various religions would take hold. The violent leaders might then be controlled or re-educated. The lessons of history show that it will probably take centuries to educate the people to the ideas of democracy and to shed their millennium old beliefs. Both history and psychology tell us that people generally don't like to be conquered, especially those in the ruling classes. The result of Bush's invasion was a huge negative reaction, not only in Iraq and the Moslem world, but in the non-Muslim world as well. Recruits to the terrorists increased, jihadists attacked more countries, anti-Western feelings increased and the U.S was weakened both financially, and in its ability to use any power that it might have had previously. Truly, those who do not understand history are condemned to repeat the errors in the use of power that history repeats endlessly. The conqueror so often ends as the conquered, either in the loss of power or prestige.

There is more than the historical event that is important. Even more important is how it impacted the future. For example, is France, or Europe, or the world, a better place because of Napoleon's impact as a ruler? He killed off about 6 million people, 1-1/2 million from his own armies. Was that bad because of the total number of deaths or was it good for population control? His structure of laws was certainly a positive. The Napoleonic Code is the legal model for many countries. It codified laws so that the people now knew their bounds and that they had equality before the law. His negative impact on monarchies may have aided the spread of democracy. The United States probably gained more than any country because of the Louisiana Purchase which allowed the United States to expand westward.

He sponsored art, and stole art. He sponsored scientific inquiry. He instituted the metric system. He increased the separation of church and state.

Again, on the negative side, his was a rather totalitarian government. There was also the scope of his wars that went far beyond the more typical two country wars. He also widened the scope of battle from merely killing soldiers, to devastating the civilian population that might help to support their army.

So the 'truth' of one's evaluation of Napoleon depends upon which factors weigh heavier on the balance scale of ethical and political achievements.

When we want to change things for the better, we must be well-versed in what has happened in the past and what stumbling blocks may fall in our path. No need to reinvent the wheel. It is seldom that a new idea arrives from a virgin birth. It usually has ancestors and relatives that will give us a clue. History shows us that the greatest atrocities are fueled by non-provable assumptions or the drive for power by tyrants.

SCIENCE AND DEMOCRACY ARE SIAMESE TWINS

Science can't tell us if there is life after death, but it can criticize some of the evidence for it. For example the out-of-body experiences or sometimes observed death-bed experience of seeing a tunnel of light with a relative or holy person waiting for us can be duplicated by stimulating certain areas of the brain. The theory of an instantaneous creation in 4004 BCE is questioned by the huge amount of evidence for evolution-- and that life, of some sort, having flowed for eons. Accepted stories of world-wide flooding a few thousand years ago is countered by geologic and paleontological evidence showing that it never happened, and by historical evidence indicating that the Biblical story was probably adapted from other flood stories, like the one found in the Epic of Gilgamesh. And the Koranic flood story was taken from the Bible.

So, while one value of science is to be critical of all theories, both past and present, and both scientific and ephemeral, it does imbue us with values that help us to search for certainty—or at least probabilities. Its values include seeking demonstrable truth, criticism of scientific and non-scientific ideas, doubting the certainty of beliefs, open dialogue between an antagonistic advocate for a theory, an honesty that follows the facts wherever they may lead, and a tolerance for views with conflicting but verifiable evidence. These values give us a new concept of probability, of pragmatism.

We can see similarities between the pragmatism of democracy and the pragmatism of science. Both require educated practitioners. Both are looking for the best solution. Both have huge numbers of variables that need to be sorted out, eliminated or emphasized. Both should include a spirit of tolerance for other verifiable ideas. Both require freedom of speech. Both should be unimpeded by prejudicial ideas from philosophies and religions that preclude their verification.

What we call democracies may choose to be totally religious. Look at Iran and Iraq. And certainly, the philosophies of the Enlightenment were instrumental in the forging of the American and French democracies. What I am trying to illustrate is that if an idea isn't verifiable it isn't of much use in science or in a pragmatic democracy. Has Islam made Iraq or Iran's people better off in terms of economic efficiency and happiness? Has it given the people freedom or has it suppressed it?

Of course, you have to question how much freedom is actually good. The Dutch allowed prostitution and many drugs, but that freedom, or license-- we should probably say, brought some problems. Other criminal behavior, such as robbery, came along with it. So, the government reined in some of the freedoms for the good of the society. Sociologically those freedoms were negative for the greater society. So the laws have now been adjusted. Another illustration is the prostitution which was allowed in Norway. It brought in prostitutes from Russia, Nigeria and East Europe. AIDS increased, so did drug usage. So it clamped down on the sex shoppers, the Johns. Many prostitutes left and carried with them the problems they had brought.

The government of Iraq is undeniably Muslim. The problems of sitting enough Sunnis as Shias in the National Assembly was a major task of government. It didn't work. The Sunnis, who had prospered under Saddam Hussein, found themselves severely prejudiced against in most areas of their lives. The Shi idea of religion was primary. There are some similarities in Israel, where the Ultra-Orthodox often hold the more liberal Jews hostage. And look at America where George W. Bush's religious views and those of his Evangelical supporters pushed abstinence as the way to curb AIDS in Africa and the way to reduce pregnancies at home. Research showed that it didn't work—and it had far more negative effects than would have supplying condoms. The God-based value assumptions of Bush versus the self-centered assumptions of most Africans did not jibe in this area!

Philosophical ideas can also get in the way of democracy and science. Look at Marx's Communism in the Soviet Union and in China. Any idea of democratic elections was overruled by the essential and ultimate goal of Communism. Single party rule is not democratic. Democratic voting has never chosen a total Communist government. On the other hand, Socialism, or I should say the welfare state, has been chosen by some countries in democratic elections.

Ideas gleaned from Rousseau, on the natural goodness of children and a basic feeling of equality, or the idea that science is necessary for a utopian society, as Bacon thought, may find their way into guiding principles of a nation's political or economic thinking.

Communism hasn't worked as an economic system based on totalitarian central planning. It held the Soviet Union back. But China's totalitarian regime allowed for some free enterprise and its economy rolled upward—aided by the totalitarian agenda to reduce its population. As we look at freedoms, time will tell if they work.

Deregulating airlines worked for the consumers, but many airlines went bankrupt. A lack of regulating of home financing, business loans and investing, along with an excess of people who were not trained for the available jobs or who didn't want to work, led to the world-wide recession of 2008. Countries may learn from their mistakes. That is where democracy relies on science and intelligent observation.

Economics looks at itself as a science, but how verifiable and predictive is it today? How much regulation of investment firms is optimal? How much money should investors be allowed to borrow? What level of borrowing by a government is optimal? Maximal? What is the optimal level of taxation on income? On sales? On food? How much federal annual income should be spent on education? On infrastructure repair? These are not nearly as verifiable as how much fluorine should be in the tap water or how many trans-fats should be allowed in the nation's cookies.

On every level of a democratic society there must be the unfettered ability to question everything. When your society prevents you from reasoning it is the Grim Reaper burying progress. When you stop questioning you are intellectually dead and are merely waiting for the Reaper's scythe. Whenever citizens are prevented from questioning their government, discussing global warming, bantering about the Big Bang, arguing about abortion, or evaluating the pros and cons of the advantages of evolution--the society, as well as its empirical and historical underpinnings, are compromised. And this is not an area where compromise is acceptable.

EVOLUTION

What about Charles Darwin's and Alfred Wallace's theory of evolution as history? Is it history or science or both? As you know, for nearly two hundred years scientists and religionists have grappled with the theory of evolution. Evolution is history but it is also science because we have the items we talk about—trilobites, dinosaurs, skeletons of pre-*homo sapiens*, and other fossils. It's difficult for many to understand that all plants and animals have a common ancestor. But since scientific truth is actually more difficult to believe than a religious myth, we often choose the myth. Can you imagine ten trillion galaxies each with millions or billions of suns and probably hundreds of billions of planets? It is beyond our comprehension! It's simpler to believe that only our flat world exists and that it was created in six days. Six we can understand, infinity we can't.

The scientific theory of evolution is often misunderstood by non-scientists. While outside of science, the word 'theory' generally means 'speculation' or 'conjecture', such as that "I have a theory about how to win at blackjack." So in the general sense it is an hypothesis, not yet proven. However, the meaning in science of the word "theory" means "a conclusion, based on empirical facts, that has been tested or is generally accepted and which can be used to make predictions in the areas studied by the various sciences.' So Einstein's theories of relativity are the best conclusions known for explaining a number of occurrences in the field of physics. And, the theory of evolution is the best conclusion for explaining the development of flora and fauna over the history of life on this planet. So, in the scientific fields, 'theory' does not mean an unproven hypothesis, but is rather a proven hypothesis. Consequently, in scientific terms, evolution has moved from a 'what if' hypothesis to an 'it is' theory.

The theory of evolution started with looking at the variation of animals and how the more primitive animals were found in the earlier geological strata. It moved on to classifying the various types of animals from the single celled amoebas to mammals, and since humans were doing the classifying we decided that we were the most intelligent. Along the way it was obvious that millions of species had died out. Saber tooth cats and tyrannosaurus now only inhabit museums. We thought we had pretty well stopped evolving, although some have postulated that our human successors will be large brained, large headed, small bodied humans. So we are probably just another link, not the end of the chain.

Of course, we can't predict which way we will actually evolve, or whether global warming, a more deadly pandemic, or nuclear warfare will bring our evolution to an abrupt end. But we can look backward and see that evolution is not really by chance. The accidents that happen through mutations and other means will tend to remain if they help the species, or they will die out if they don't.

The study of evolution may have developed with Darwin's and Wallace's theories but it has been verified by studies in a number of sciences. We first saw increasing complexity of organisms in succeeding strata of geological deposits. Wherever we looked we saw more complex development as the millions of years rolled on. As the sciences of paleontology and anthropology developed, we looked at the human forerunners, their use of tools, their increasing brain size and complexity. We can see how common ancient ancestors sired species that evolved in different directions than we did. Paranthropus, was once thought to be somewhere in our evolutionary trail, now we find he was not. He died out while our ancestors continued to evolve along the path that led to us, and we too are evolving as long as we can keep our planet species friendly—controlling our ecology.

New sciences have joined the hunt to clarify and deepen our understanding of the fact of evolution. We no longer need to look only at skulls and skeletons with the physical anthropologists, we can trace the genetic trail from the earliest times by having the neuro-geneticists analyzing DNA and genes. We can analyze the skulls for brain form and complexity with the paleo-neurologists. Science after science confirms the empirical findings of our multi-million-year descent to who we are today.

As the human genome is studied it became clear that we are still evolving. During the last 15,000 years there have been many changes. The genes that show this evolutionary change include those genes responsible for the senses of taste and smell, digestion, bone structure, skin color and brain function. Darwin's idea of natural selection is still at work. In making the transition from hunter-gatherers to farmers about 5000 to 7000 years ago it seems that some traits were more desirable than others. For example, Europeans developed the ability to digest milk in adulthood—because animal milk was a diet staple. Many humans still don't have this genetic ability.

While some think that evolution and religion are mutually exclusive, many religious believers reason that evolution is true. It is the divine plan of God. This divine plan obviously assumes that at some point in the evolutionary process, God put a soul into his advanced creations and we had humanity—we were thus made in the Image of God. Some religious scientists believe that understanding the idea of evolution is the key to affirming our faith in God. And St. Paul wrote in Romans 8:22 that 'We know that the whole creation has been groaning, as in the pains of childbirth, right up to the present time.'

From Pope Pius XII in 1950 to Pope John Paul in 1996, the popes have held that even though evolution is no longer merely a hypothesis, we must believe Catholic tradition which holds that at some point God created and infused the soul.

In a different vein, in 2007 Pope Benedict wrote that 'Science has increased our knowledge of life's origins, but the theory of evolution is not completely provable because mutations over the millennia cannot be reproduced in the laboratory.' (Schoepfung und Evolution [Creation and Evolution] Sankt Ulrich, 2007) He concluded that the immense time span that evolution covers made it impossible to conduct experiments in a controlled environment to finally verify or disprove the theory. 'We cannot haul 10,000 generations into the laboratory,' he said.

 But by his reasoning we would also have to bring his religious scriptures into the laboratory and re-enact the whole Biblical story, both the Old and the New Testaments. Then when he talks about the huge time-span covered by evolution theory, he doesn't criticize his own beliefs which cover only a few thousand years of history. How might he criticize his own beliefs in a 'controlled environment?' The Pope's remarks were consistent with one of his most important themes, that faith and reason are interdependent. He said that 'science has opened up large dimensions of reason and thus brought us new insights, but in the joy at the extent of its discoveries, it tends to take away from us dimensions of reason that we still need.' You have to admit that the human power of being able to reason is critical to our humanness. And just because we don't understand it, it doesn't mean that it isn't true.

 But that goes for both uneducated people not believing in science just as much as it does for atheists not believing in a creating god. That opens up the question as to whether we can actually reason. Are we merely reacting to psychological stimuli? Are we merely trying to rationalize our beliefs in our myths by finding any possible reasons to make them sound plausible to our doubting minds?

The Pope said that science has opened up large dimensions of reason ... and thus brought us new insights. Remember that Pope Benedict had been a theology professor. He reminded us that pure reason allows us to go beyond the findings of science. Science cannot answer the great questions of where we and the world came from and where we are going. He is in the mainstream of Catholics, Orthodox and Protestants, in his belief that God's process of creation is done through evolution.

But the findings of evolution show that evolutionary changes don't always go in a positive direction, sometimes they go backwards. These mutations may occur very slowly in terms of taking millions of years. And the Pope doesn't seem to understand that evolution doesn't always occur through purely random selection. He assumes there is a conflict between theology and science and that theology wins. But he doesn't really understand what evolutionary biology has discovered. His knowledge is a half century or more behind what science has found out. So while he acknowledges the findings of science, including those related to the science of evolution, he sets up a straw man from the early 1900s, then knocks it down with reasoning from the 14th century. I wonder if Aquinas would agree with Benedict today if he had access to today's scientific findings. The point is that making up a myth, like religions continually do, does not explain the formation of the universe, the world, evolution, or us. We are better off intellectually if we just say 'we don't know' or if we wait for a more probable theory. The myth of the Mid-East god is no explanation at all for an educated person.

Why is the reasoning power of Catholic popes and theologians held in so much higher esteem than the reasoning power of non-theistic philosophers or of thinkers in other religions? Was Maimonides really the rational inferior to Augustine or Avicenna or Bertrand Russell? And you realize that we are not the end point of evolution. Assuming that we can avoid annihilating our race, which is a huge assumption, somewhere in the future there may be a race of people that can reason effectively and will have the evidence of far more advanced science, than we do, to help them with their reasoning. It's hard for many to understand that we are not the ultimate end-point for evolution.

In fact, if we can avoid the human-caused Armageddon, there will be no end to evolution until the planet is destroyed by a giant asteroid or is sucked into the sun by a slowing of the Earth's speed—or the gasses of the sun are exhausted and we freeze!

It is very scary to think of that ultimate end. Whether we question the Armageddon of Revelation or the Armageddon of Nature we must be afraid for our species and our world. It is no wonder that Darwin put off publishing 'The Origin of the Species' for twenty years. He knew it would look like he was murdering God—and "theo-cide" has never been popular with the masses. But then since the dawn of science and critical thinking, the death of the God concept has been gaining momentum with the educated elite.

ACCEPTING OUR KNOWLEDGE FROM AUTHORITY

The simplest evidence comes from authority. Our parents and teachers were our earliest sources of 'absolute truth.' This is where we learn to believe in Santa Claus and the Easter Bunny. Mothers tell daughters that the way to a man's heart is through his stomach. If they asked their fathers the organ with the direct connection to the heart is several inches below the stomach, and is outside of the abdominal cavity.

Our parents convince us of the existence of Santa Claus, the Easter Bunny and the Tooth Fairy. By the time we are 10 we have lost our belief in the Easter Bunny and the Tooth Fairy. By 20 we probably have changed our belief about Santa, but we don't want to give up our adult myth of a god who will greet us after our death.

We need to examine the credentials of the authority we are asked to believe, and look for any inconsistencies in its actions and the intentions of that authority. If your mother told you there was a special bunny hiding eggs early on Easter morning or a tooth fairy leaving money under your pillow for every baby tooth you lost, we can certainly understand that in her misrepresentation of reality, she had good intentions. But when we have a national leader who lies to us about why we are going to war, that's a bit more serious and more costly. What if we have a well-intentioned person who is either misinformed or is hearing a voice from a psychotic source, or we have a power-hungry person who seeks the esteem of those who see him as holy? Or maybe that authority comes from people like Mark Twain who said 'When I was younger, I could remember anything, whether it happened or not.'

When President Bush told his Secretary of State and the American people that there were weapons of mass destruction in Iraq—we believed our President because he was in the major position of authority. But he was wrong, as authoritarian sources often are.

AUTHORITY FROM RELIGIOUS MENTORS

When suicide bombers believe that they will be greeted in heaven by 70 virgins—who told them that and on what authority? The word used for 'virgins' has also been translated as 'maidens' and 'raisins.' Apparently, raisins were a great delicacy for Arabs when the hadiths were written. Would these young people still die for a bunch of dried grapes? But some of the hadiths mention that men will have 70 wives in Paradise. So who, or what, do you believe?

If there is a god, would the ultimate authority be that Supreme Being's revelations in the Avestas of the Zoroastrians, the Old Testament of the Christians, the Tanakh of the Jews, the New Testament of the Christians, the Qur'an of the Muslims, the Book of Mormon of the Church of Jesus Christ of Latter Day Saints, the sacred scriptures of Baha'u'llah of the Bahai faith, and perhaps the 'ruti' texts of Hinduism which were whispered by the wind to Brahmin priests and might be considered to be from the Infinite. Are these all revelations from the same god? Or is only one of these revelations true?

These all started as oral traditions handed down from the person God chose to be the recipient of His holy word such as Moses, Paul, or Muhammad. Eventually they were written. Some people question whether God chose the best writers for his revelations. Perhaps Sophocles, or if we wanted more humor, Aristophanes would have been better choices. Or if he wanted it easy to read for the popes—Dante could have been chosen.

But most of these authoritative writings were passed by word of mouth for hundreds of years before they were written. The Dead Sea Scrolls of the Essenes about 200 BCE and the Mishnah of Rabbi Judah in about 200 AD give us the Jewish tradition. The gospels and the letters of Paul give us the start of Christian tradition sometime after 50 AD. But the Qur'an was written during the early years of the Muslim religion.

But there are many other texts that are sometimes even more important than the holy scriptures for some people. When the Pope speaks *ex cathedra* his pronouncements become law for Catholics. Teachers in all religions have interpreted, embellished and changed the direction of the original revelations. The more years that have elapsed, the more changes develop. Often a majority of the rulers of a religion make a decision that redirects the religion. The church councils of the Catholic Church are examples. The writings of Maimonides gave Jews an enhanced view of their religion. In Islam, the Sunnis have followed the teachings of the caliphate while the Shia say they hold true to Muhammad's teachings. But the Sunnis don't see the Shia as true Muslims. New teachings or emphases are found in every religion.

Of course, these new directions are not accepted by all. The letters of Paul, although accepted as dogma by most Christians, are not accepted by all of them. Thomas Jefferson, as an example, deleted them from his views of New Testament ethics. Since Paul's approach to religion was Greek, and he never met Jesus, some think that his teachings don't reflect the Master. In fact, there are those who argue that without Paul, the sect of Jesus would have remained in the Jewish religion. So perhaps the religion should be called Paulianity rather than Christianity.

From an historical point of view, an oral or written text becomes scripture when a group of people begin to treat it as such, when they accept it as either being from the supernatural, as with Christians, Muslims and Zoroastrians, or as being ultimately true, as in the philosophies of Siddhartha Gautama, Lao Tzu or Confucius. In any case, to be true scriptures they must be venerated and viewed as absolute truth.

Some ask why did God give people intelligence—if not to use it? If God only wanted non-thinking obedience, He would have made us all Pavlovian dogs!

We can also see the leaders of many sects who take a small bit of a scripture, then use it to rile the unthinking rabble to kill those of different beliefs. Or, there are those who call on the faithful for money to line their own pockets with diamonds, as a way for the donors to enter the Pearly Gates.

We Westerners used to believe in witches and astrology. Certainly, fewer people believe these now. We need schools that will teach our future citizens to be able to think effectively using the tools of logic and science. Every source of authority must be questioned. Whether it is the Bible or Koran toting, fire-breathing holier-than-thou ministers, or the omniscient and charitable political leaders promising us tax cuts, we must analyze and evaluate the historical and economic beliefs and promises. If we don't do it effectively, we become the losers. But I don't think the people of most countries are ready for it. I have to agree with Einstein when he said 'Only two things are infinite, the universe and human stupidity, and I'm not sure about the former.'

There's the other factor-- when you know everything, you lose your ability to be tolerant.

But tolerance may be overemphasized. We shouldn't be tolerant of suicide bombers or rapists or unethical politicians or religious leaders who foster violence rather than mercy. There is no question that people who cloak themselves in the robe of religion are too often shielded from criticism. Scriptures often give many people a mantle of invulnerability and a reason for governments to follow their wishes. Why should churches get preferential tax treatment that other groups doing good works are denied. Why should anyone who calls himself a minister or priest get all of the advantages of the major religions. When there is a separation of church and state, why are religions allowed to put their beliefs into the classrooms and onto their coins? Why don't we just emphasize the Golden Rule?

Why allow churches to be sanctuaries for those who have broken the law, particularly illegal aliens. Why is a church allowed to supersede society's laws? Even when you supposedly have a separation of church and state, the church calls the shots! Why is a politically responsible society held captive by a group whose claim to legitimacy is based on non-provable assumptions without verifiable historical evidence?

And as we have already mentioned, when a religion says that its beliefs require that it use a drug that society has outlawed, it can do it—because it is a religion. (Gonzales v. O Centro [2006] op. cit.)

Is there anything more counterproductive to an effective society than the certainty of religions. Knowing for certain what happens after death and how the world was developed is an appealing desire, but why believe it just because some shepherd said so a thousand or more years ago? And yet religions strongly shape political decisions in the US, both national and international decisions. Why do people continue to believe in the conflicting claims of unproven authorities when they have a better way towards truth.

Strongly religious countries often put religion into the classrooms. They keep trying to do it in the U.S., but the courts often block it. But in Norway, with its state religion, they put a required class on religion in the schools, but some humanist parents fought the requirement in the courts. They lost at every court level in Norway so they took it to the EU'S Court of Human Rights in Strasbourg and finally won in 2007. It took ten years of court fights, but they defeated the authority of the state in this instance.

It's lucky for us that some people have a direct line to the Almighty—Pat Robertson, Osama bin Ladin, George Bush, Pope Benedict, or Iran's Ayatollah Ali Khamenei. By following any of them we know what God wants us to do and what political approach to follow.

Since so many people have the direct line to God and they are all saying He wants different things, is this proof for polytheism? Are there many gods talking to many people giving them different information? Maybe the ancient Greeks were right!

But as long as we are assuming, let's just assume a monotheistic god. Then we might ask if is it God's will that hurricanes and earthquakes happen, but not that some wars are started. It may be God's will to start a war, or to fight against that war. It is God's will that we die of diabetes but against God's will to develop stem cell research that might cure the disease. It is against God's will to commit suicide, but it is OK to be a suicide bomber, a Christian martyr, or to give one's life for a cause. Is it God's will that millions of children starve to death every year, but against God's will to use contraception or abortion to stop their birth so that they won't suffer? How do we, with our finite minds, sort out the reasoning of the Infinite? How can we know who has the direct pipeline to God? Within the same religion we have opposing 'truths' as to what God wants us to do.

After Hurricane Katrina devastated New Orleans the Columbia Christians for Life announced that it was God's punishment because there were five abortion clinics in the area. God had even provided a proof. Radar photos from above the hurricane looked like a fetus. The Reverend Franklin Graham, saw it in more general terms as a punishment for the non-Christian sinning, sexual perversion and the use of voodooism, saying that 'There's been Satanic worship in New Orleans. There's been sexual perversion. God is going to use that storm to bring a revival. God has a plan. God has a purpose.'

Is it more likely that God was upset with the city because its professional football team was called the Saints. And the Pope hadn't canonized them. But seriously some say that America has replaced the Jews as the chosen people of God? Many think so. Who else is fighting to preserve those Christian values that are not found in the Bible—like democracy, the prohibition of contraception, abortion, nudity and stem cell research? If God didn't want these possibilities to limit population and heal the sick, why did He allow them to be discovered?

Quite a number of us have heard it as an excuse for not believing in God or as a snide comment suggesting that Christians are weak and have invented a 'crutch' named Jesus to lean on. And maybe it would have been necessary to invent God. But just because God might be a necessity, doesn't mean that humans invented Him. It simply means that God created that need in us. Man having a need for God isn't proof that God doesn't exist,

Let's look at this 'need thing' another way. I need food and, if food didn't exist, I'd need to either invent it or find an alternative pretty soon. But, just because we need food doesn't mean we invented it, does it? The food was there before we were, and we simply used it to our best advantage. The same is true of all the Earth's resources although we constantly bicker about their best use. God is there for us to use to our best advantage. He even gives us guidance on how to 'use' Him correctly and efficiently.

POLITICAL AUTHORITIES

Thomas Jefferson told us in his Declaration of Independence that we were all created equal. He didn't believe it, but he believed that we must be independent of England. About a third of Americans were convinced and took up arms. As mentioned, George W. Bush told us that Saddam Hussein had weapons of mass destruction, so we didn't object to his attacking Iraq--for a while. James Polk wanted Texas and California, it was the "manifest destiny" of the United States, so he told us that Mexican troops had fired on Americans. He told others that a Catholic country next door would be a problem for our mainly Protestant country.

IGNORANT OR PROPAGANDA LOUDMOUTHS WITH MEDIA ACCESS

When you have access to radio, television or the social media you can influence a large number of uninformed or ignorant people. And, if they hear it enough times they will believe it--in fact, one time may be enough. What are the motivations of these missionaries of myths? Power is the major motivator--being able to have a large number of followers. QAnon and the anti-vaxxer sites are examples. Often it is that drive for power combined with financial gain. Many on the Rupert Murdock news outlets must deliver the type of propaganda that he wants in order to be employed. And, the higher your ratings, the higher your salary.

So much for believing in authority as a path to truth!

PERSONAL EXPERIENCE

What should I believe? If I say that I have seen a flying saucer, I believe it. If I have had a mystical experience with God, I believe it. If I feel that I have left my body and done astral traveling, I believe it. If I have seen a ghost, I believe it. If I put a straight stick in the water and the stick now appears bent from the waterline, do I believe that it has actually bent or do I look for another explanation, such as the refraction of light through the water. What I experience is that the sun goes around the earth from east to west. What I observe from the ground is that the earth is flat. What I observe from space is that the earth is more like a round ball.

Yet many such experiences find their way into religion. Did Saul of Tarsus actually have the experience he said he had on the road to Damascus? When we see the magic or illusions of David Copperfield, millions of us see it at the same time. His most famous feats include making the Statue of Liberty disappear, flying over the Grand Canyon, and walking through the Great Wall of China. We assume that it is illusion, because he says it is. But what of others who claim to have experienced or done things that we haven't seen?

As said earlier, we often mistake our feelings for thinking. And I think we often experience our sensations as being true representations of objective reality.

Many people have had experiences in which they believe they have experienced ultimate reality. This is called a mystical experience. Usually that ultimate reality is the supernatural. Sometimes it is a reaching out to a theistic God. Sometimes it is an experience of going deeper into one's self and feeling a pantheistic experience—where god is the totality of the universe, as in the tradition of the Hindu religion. Sometimes it is an experience of the oneness of nature and is not thought of as a religious experience. Nothing is more real to these people that their experience. But is it an experience with God or a blip in one's brain?

LSD and mescaline were once thought by some to be able to give some people this mystical experience. However, people who say they have had the mystical experience and have had an experience under the influence of a psychedelic drug, say that they aren't the same. So truth does not depend on your opinion. (Zaehner, R. C. Mysticism Sacred and Profane: An Inquiry into Some Varieties of Praternatural Experience. London: Oxford University Press. 1973.)

FAITH

Science deals with things that can be seen and measured—but faith, as St. Paul wrote in Hebrews 11:1, 'is the substance of things hoped for, the evidence of things not seen.' So faith is invisible. But few ask for evidence when they have faith and hope. Why should we leave our feather bed of emotional contentment for a world of prickly facts that just torment our minds. Certainly, the truth hurts! Much of what we do relies on faith. You have faith that when you get in your car you will not have an accident. Usually your faith is affirmed. But what if yesterday your car didn't start and your mechanic told you that the fuel line was clogged but he couldn't fix it until tomorrow. If you have faith that your car will still start today before the fuel line is unclogged, your faith has been placed in an impossibility.

You have faith when you go to work that you will get your paycheck, that you will not be terminated and that there will be money for your pension when you retire. Generally, these happen, but not always. In these instances, you have some historical evidence to back up your faith. For example, the company has been in business for a hundred years and has always fulfilled its contract with its employees. But when you see giant corporations like Enron or WorldCom and many of the major airlines in bankruptcy and many major companies downsizing, often without adequate pension reserves, your faith may be misplaced. If you had lived in New Orleans a year before Katrina struck would you have made certain that you had ample flood insurance that was guaranteed to pay off in case of a hurricane? Most people didn't. Did the people working in the Twin Towers on the morning of 9/11 have faith that they would return home safely that night?

Some of the things in which we put our faith are highly probable. The Twin Towers employees were almost certainly going home that evening. New Orleans residents did not have nearly the same chance of escaping a hurricane, since hurricanes are a fact of life in the Gulf of Mexico and global warming was making them more frequent and more potent.

Traveling a mile on a commercial jet liner is much safer than traveling a mile in a car. But is it possible that traveling a mile on Singapore Airlines is safer than on a transatlantic flight of an American or British airliner because of the terrorist threats?

If the president of a major country says that flying is safe, is that a more likely possibility than when a minister says that the Bible is literally true? When a university biologist says I believe in a creating God, is that more likely to be true than when another university biologist says that I don't believe in a creating God?

In 2005 the Thai Prime Minister, Thaksin Shinawatra refused to answer questions from the press because Mercury was in a line with his star—and Mercury is not good. So, a belief in astrology was more important than freedom of the press.

When you have faith that God is on your side you can do anything—judge and punish in an inquisition, kill harmless civilians in a marketplace, invade sovereign lands, kill doctors who perform abortions, use capital punishment, or use torture as a means of religious conversion.

The danger, as I see it, is when people place their faith in possibilities that have no other grounds than that they want it to be true. Hope and faith often give us a path to follow and a certainty of complacency. But shall we base the only life we will ever have on the beliefs inculcated by our parents', or shall we seek more probable paths to truth. Shall we question our world, our thoughts, our behavior? Shall we actively seek truth in our questioning and experiencing of our world. Shall we converse with intelligent people and study the great literature of our sages? Or shall we wrap ourselves in the cloak of complacency, snuggle into our easy chair, and let an idiot box entertain us?

The ideas I have just enumerated are not mine alone. Roger Bacon, the 13th Century British philosopher said 'There are four chief obstacles in grasping truth ... namely, submission to faulty and unworthy authority, influence of custom, popular prejudice, and the concealment of our own ignorance accompanied by an ostentatious display of our knowledge.'

REASON

Some people can think their way into a code of values, but generally our values are ingrained in us from our childhood by our families, churches and societies. Europeans generally abhor capital punishment, Americans believe it is a necessity. Americans hold it sacred to carry a firearm and a duty to use it, but the baring of a breast is a national disgrace. Unthinking and misguided Europeans think the body is to be enjoyed and shudder at the possibility of being a gun toting Wyatt Earp. The sins of one nation are the prides of another.

Is the major ingredient of faith the ability to reason? Does Allah give us only the ability to believe but not to understand more deeply—or even the ability to question, to make our faith deeper. Or has He made us in his merciful image, able to think freely and to reason effectively?

Thomas Aquinas wrote that faith cannot be irrational. God does not contradict Himself—what He teaches through revelation does not conflict with the truths that humans can reason for themselves. Aquinas admired and echoed the ancient Greeks and the Moslem scholars of his day.

Not all great thinkers believe that the reasoning mind is the best source of knowledge and solace. Blaise Pascal preferred the reasons of the heart to the reasons of the mind, so for him it was 'feelings' over 'philosophy.' But John Locke, Thomas Hobbes and David Hume found the mind primary. And if, as the Christians say, the mind is what the Bible calls the Image of God, then, can these skeptics be right. Would the mind of God tell us that there is no God?'

What kinds of cognition and modes of thinking may affect our mental or physical health? The founder of rational-emotive-behavior therapy, Albert Ellis, pointed out that non-rational thought was the factor leading to negative mood reactions and various biological or psychological symptoms. So, the job of a therapist is to make the client confront his non-rational thoughts then replace them with rational thinking.

If we believe that non-rational thoughts are among the reasons that lead to negative moods and to various biological or psychological symptoms, we must change them with our reasoning processes. When we rationally develop our thoughts, we will come up with satisfying life philosophies and will choose more satisfying work and better social relationships. We will then be happier and physically and mentally happier. This is what a large part of what our discussion is about—understanding our values better and making us think through our life choices.

As I will continue to repeat, we are psychological not logical. What we 'feel' is more important in our beliefs than what we 'reason.' The mystical experience of union with the Infinite, as Theresa of Avila and so many others have experienced, is felt to be real. From Sufis dancing their way to a transcendent state to an evangelical experiencing the Holy Spirit, then speaking in tongues, there is nothing more real than the mystical experience—the union with the eternal, the Supernatural, God. Yet most people have not had this all-encompassing experience so they yearn for the hereafter—the heaven of the Christians, the paradise of the Moslems, Gan Eden of the Jews, the pure land of some theistic Buddhists, the House of Song of the Zoroastrians, the land on the other side of the River Styx for the ancient Egyptians.

Black Lives Matter is certainly correct, that there has been an anti-Black racism in America They are correct in that some police officers are racist and wear heavy badges. They have a right to be emotional about those situations. They may know that more Whites are killed by police, although at a lower percent of the population than Blacks. But they seem to overlook the fact that over 90% of Black murder victims are killed by Blacks. Do their lives matter too? Might they spend as much time attempting to reduce the Black murder rate and Black criminality? But that would take. much more research as to how, and much more work than merely demonstrating when a Black man is killed while committing a crime or resisting arrest. An emotional appeal is simple to organize and gets good press. It is necessary, but it doesn't go very far in fixing the real problem. Will defunding the police really save the lives of innocent Black citizens? An intellectual approach might be to attempt to reduce the criminality of the society, while finding police recruits with less violent tendencies--and finding non-lethal effective weapons that will subdue criminals.

Greta Thunberg's Extinction Rebellion reached far more people. Greta even spoke to the United Nations. Many nations were already concerned. Donald Trump and Brazil's President Bolsonaro denied it, as did many legislators. How could it be true if it was bad for the oil and coal industries? The emotional pleas are to reduce the fossil fuel us by people. Nobody thinks about reducing the number of people! Maybe Mother Nature is trying to tell us something with her pandemics, famine-producing droughts, and floods. We are alerted by the demonstrations of the young, but nobody is attempting to solve the underlying problems!

If you have ever had a session with a therapist, you probably know that it is a common question for a therapist to ask 'how do you feel about that,' when discussing a problem. Psychologists generally believe that most of us are 'feelers' rather than 'philosophizers.'

That is why it is so important to understand that we commonly 'mistake our feelings for thinking.' Over and over again, in discussing how we come up with our values, we encounter people not only clinging to their pasts, but afraid to critically evaluate them. They should all become philosophers so that they will be more critical. Perhaps we shouldn't care about what their eventual beliefs are, just as long as they arrive at them by critical thinking.

THE PROCESS OF REASONING

If you plan on using your ability to reason you must understand that you can't argue about basic assumptions, because they are only assumed. Then you must use the best evidence available. The hard sciences like chemistry and physics are more verifiable than the softer sciences of psychology, sociology and economics. But these are generally more verifiable than historical evidence. And history, at least more recent history, is more likely to have been more complete and documented than ancient history. And traditional beliefs, rules from authority, or our personal experience are all less likely to be adequately verifiable.

Once we have the evidence, we have to follow the rules of logic. We need both. If we start with evidence that is less likely to be true, we don't have a chance of logically coming to a true conclusion.

If I say that 'Joe is a giraffe' and 'all giraffes are honest' therefore 'Joe is honest.' The conclusion may be logically valid, but the premises are meaningless so the conclusion doesn't conclude anything real. But if I say 'Reverend Smith is a religious leader' then I say 'all religious leaders are honest' I must conclude that 'Reverend Smith is honest.' But are all religious leaders honest? No. Is Reverend Smith actually a religious leader? How do we define 'religious leader'? Must he have a following of a thousand people to be considered to be a leader? Must he be in one of the five major religions? What if he is an Inca sun worshipper with only two followers? Is he religious? Is he a leader?

When the tsunami hit Thailand one person said it was the will of God. Another said it was the result of an undersea volcano erupting that caused a tidal wave. Some may combine the two saying that God made the volcano erupt. What evidence do we have for either statement?

If we are going to think logically, philosophy has shown us how. We first start with probabilities, and if necessary, definitions. That is inductive logic. Then we argue according to deductive logic. There are a number of rules for this.

What if we want to prove that humans are generally directed by a drive for power? How would we define humans? Well, they have 46 chromosomes.

But some have 45 and some have 47 or 48. On the other hand, guppies have 46 chromosomes. So, should we accept these fish as part of the human race? Are chimps close enough, with 48 chromosomes, that we should include them? Should we define humans by their IQ? But some animals will score higher than some people. So, shall we bring the animals into the human group or drop some people out of it? Or is humanness all about whether we have souls? If so, we are not using empirical or historical evidence or even personal experience. It has to be based on some monotheistic God related basic assumptions.

Next, we would have to define 'power.' We might define it as power over others or power to accomplish something. Then we would have to do a psycho-social study to determine if all, none, or some humans demonstrated one or the other types of power, and if so, how much.

So saying that people are driven by power is not a simple proposition, nor is it easy to determine the probability of it being true.

So when making a logical statement we have to define our terms. Does God exist? Exactly what do I mean by God? Do I mean a merciful or vengeful monotheistic God, a deistic being who is unconcerned with the world, a pantheistic idea that God is everywhere and is not judgmental. Or do I have some other idea. So, if you and I are discussing God, we had better be on the same page— 'Almightingly' speaking.

 Yet people can take a much more difficult concept, that there is a God, and accept it without question. Why? Because we are psychological, not logical. We want simple explanations for complicated questions and problems. If we accept that there is a creating God, we can jump to the idea that morals come from that God and that eternal life comes from that same God.

 As long as we are assuming, we will have gone all the way. Now we don't have to think of us ceasing to exist. We don't have to think of where we came from, we don't have to think about what is good or bad. All we have to do is pray or meditate and go to the mosque on Friday, the synagogue on Saturday or to church on Sunday-- and our eternity is assured. But remember there are rules for meeting with God. The Muslims know that they must take their hats and shoes off. Jews leave their shoes on and most will wear a yarmulkas on their heads. Christians will wear shoes, but leave their hats off. God has strange requirements for His worship.

India for millennia had a caste system in which the level of society in which one was born defined his or her social status for a lifetime. It was an assumption based on the natural inequality of humans, sanctified by the idea of reincarnation which was part of their religion. Only after Gandhi's insistence, that those born so low that they were below a caste and were untouchable, did these 'children of God' find new hope. Gandhi formulated a new assumption based more on the democratic ideal of equality and did what he could to force an assumption of equality into a society that had assumed a basic inequality of humans. The birth of modern India and its constitution outlawed the caste system and the more mobile 'class system' of the West became a possibility. The cream was allowed, with great difficulty, to rise to the top. Fifty years after the birth of the nation a former untouchable became the president of the country. Changing basic assumptions is a difficult, if not impossible, task for us as individuals and it is even more difficult for societies.

Basic assumptions and values can vary within a family. While Osama bin Laden was responsible for the terror attacks of September 11, 2001 in New York, his half-brother Yeslam bin Laden condemned the attacks and said he issued a statement following the attacks, condemning 'all kinds of violence.' Yeslam said that Osama, who had not left Saudi Arabia to study abroad like most of his brothers, 'was more religious than the rest.' His values were different. 'Osama didn't like music or TV and banned his kids from being entertained by them,' Yeslam said. 'I grew up thinking this is weird, but he's free in his household and I'm free in mine.'

We have seen many problems in the Catholic Church because of different assumptions and points of view. U.S. Catholics have often had a conflict of values. They support their church but disapprove of the sex scandals that have afflicted many of their clergy. They often disapprove of the Pope's rules that forbid female or married clergy and many disagree with the Church's stands against homosexuality, contraception and abortion. When they withhold their contributions, the church suffers economically. While the 80 million U.S. Catholics make up only about 6% of the world's Catholics, they contribute about a third of the total of the Church's worldwide charities. Additionally, fewer women and men have the vocation to serve in religious orders. The number of nuns in 1965 was 180,000, today it is less than 80,000 and their average age is over 70. Parishes that once had two or three priests now may have none. The Irish connection has all but dried up. A great many priests were from the 'old sod.' Priests and nuns who worked for only their room and board must now be replaced by lay workers who must have living wages. That puts the squeeze on church finances. The costs of the sex scandals has averaged $700 million for each of the 3000 Catholic dioceses. Several dioceses have filed for bankruptcy.

But back to some theological questions, for those who want to think. If humans are created in the image of the Creator and are capable of both good and evil—is the creator also capable of good and evil. Or are humans not made in the image of their creator. In fact, were they created or did they merely evolve into thinking beings who, from time to time, can reason? Are they significantly separated from their Creator? If God knows what will happen in every situation, does man have the free will to do differently from what God knows will happen? Or does God merely see how man will freely choose?

Ah!, the unanswerable questions! How can we mortals understand the thinking of the Immortal? There have been attempts to answer. One is that we have free will and God sees how we will freely choose. Then there have been religions, like John Calvin's, that accept the idea of predestination, that God knows when we are born what we will do every minute and whether we will go to heaven or hell.

Our different basic assumptions push us in different directions. But perhaps with a more critical view of the evidence and the proper use of inductive and deductive logic we might come a bit closer together. And probably the basic question is whether there is a concerned Supernatural Creator involved in our lives. And, as we've said, we can only assume the correctness of our answer--whether we affirm such a being, or deny it. But it makes no sense for believers or non-believers to use unverifiable evidence or faulty logic. We are unquestionably dealing with opinions.

OPINIONS AND SEEKING EXPERTISE

We all have opinions. Are our opinions based in empirical experiments? Our view of history? Our belief that we have experienced God? And, as Upton Sinclair once noted, "It is difficult to get a man to understand something when his salary depends on his not understanding it." So, our opinions usually depend on our traditions and our economic situations. Unhappily, the proven probabilities of the various sciences seldom play a part—unless they validate our opinions.

We may be quite willing to fight to the death for our opinions. And, of course, we think that our opinions are absolute truth. I want Sam for President. But what do I really know about Sam? I know what he looks like. I know what he tells us he wants for the country. But I don't know his hidden agenda. I don't know what he has promised his big financial backers. I don't know when he is being truthful and when he is lying. But I think I know.

As a former football coach,, I found more and more problems with players and parents as they watched more televised football. They learned all their football with a remote channel changer in one hand and a beer in the other. They didn't have a clue about how to develop team cohesion, they didn't have a clue about fundamentals or what fundamentals were essential to each style of offense or defense. They had no concept about the percentages relative to the chances for success of different offensive plays or defensive stunts, they didn't understand the kicking game, they didn't know the tendencies of the opponents in every situation—but they thought they knew everything. They hadn't spent days going over the films of every game that our team and our opponents played. They hadn't seen the computer-generated scouting reports based on our hundreds of hours of film analysis. But they knew every play we should call and every defense we should execute in every situation. They thought that high school and college rules were the same as the professional rules, but there are 200 differences between college and pro rules and another 200 differences between high school and college rules.

It's like a guy I sat next to at a football game. His friend said, what play would you call. He said 'I'd pass to the right end.' The coach called a run left that gained 12 yards. What would you do now, he asked? 'I'd run up the middle.' The coach called a long pass that gained 30 yards. What now? 'I'd run left again.' The coach called a run up the middle that got them to the three yard line. What would you call now, said his friend. He replied, 'I got them this far let's see if the coach can call a play that will score.'

When generals told Donald Rumsfeld that if wanted to go war in Iraq he needed 380,000 troops. He refused and wanted to do it with 125,000. His opinion was wrong. It probably cost thousands of lives and increased the ability of jihadists to expand the conflict and increase worldwide terror.

Look at all the opinions that we hold that are not backed up by evidence. We know when a soul is put into an embryo or a baby. We know when life begins. We know when people are guilty of crimes even though there is no evidence against them. We know the best way for you to raise your kids. We know that we and our children will never be alcoholics or drug dependent. We know that when we drive fast we won't have an accident. We know we can be obese and eat lots of saturated fats, but we won't die. My goodness we're smart.

We all think we are experts on just about everything. We may admit that we don't know how to clone a cow or how to operate on a brain tumor, but we know all about sports and national and international politics.

What we need to know is how did you come to your belief in your basic assumptions? Through science? Through historical evidence? By way of some authority—parents, community, a respected person or respected people. Have you thought through them? Are you certain of what you mean when you make a statement or hold a belief?

For example, when you say abortion, do you mean any time after the sperm penetrates the ovum? Do you mean after it has attached to the uterine wall? Do you mean a cessation of pregnancy whether it was induced or natural? Do you mean only an induced cessation after the third month? Do you see any of these as acceptable, required or sinful?

When you say 'sexual relations' do you mean only sexual intercourse with the penis penetrating the vagina? Do you mean oral or anal sex? Do you mean kissing or fondling?

When you say democracy, do you mean a government like the republican form of government in most Western nations? Do you mean free trade or free speech? Do you mean a government where every citizen votes on every proposition? Would you call the government of ancient Athens a democracy when only the adult male citizens could vote?

While you can't debate basic assumptions, when you have evidence for a position it should be debated logically. There are aspects of evidence that hang from basic assumptions that can be debated. For example, while the idea of the existence of God or the supernatural origin of the scriptures can't be debated, it can be debated whether there is evidence for a world-wide flood when Noah lived. The often-accepted date of creation as 4004 BCE can certainly be debated. These are historical beliefs that can be questioned because of empirically verifiable geological evidence. Then there are philosophical or theological ideas that can be debated, such as: whether the western God is merciful or vengeful; whether the message of Christianity is that love is primary; whether one should turn the other cheek. We might also debate the Biblically based versus the non-Biblical idea that a conceived embryo has a soul and whether abortion is murder. And we might debate whether mothers seeking abortions and doctors performing them may be hassled or murdered.

SEMANTICS

The same word or paragraph doesn't always have the same meaning for the listener that was intended by the speaker. As Humpty Dumpty said to Alice 'A word means what I choose it to mean, neither more nor less. Someone might say 'I'd like to kill you.' If it is a Mossad agent he probably means to kill your physical body. But it might have been your best friend talking after you have surprised her with a practical joke. She might mean, 'I'm upset' or 'I'm really surprised.' So, 'semantics' studies the meaning of a word or term being used by a person or people. If we don't understand what another person means when they use a word, we can't discuss an issue properly. And if we don't understand what we mean by a word or an idea, we can't think clearly.

Look at the word 'anti-Semitic' which many Jews use to disparage anti-Jewish beliefs or behavior. But what does 'semitic' actually mean? The word's roots trace to Shem, Noah's middle son. It includes Jews, Christians and Muslims from the Middle East. Jesus was a Semite, so was Muhammad, but not Paul who was a Greek, but he was Jewish. But the word has been adopted by some to mean only Jews.

What about being 'black?' Barak Obama is a black man. His father was 100% black and his mother was 100% white. Is he black because it was his father's race? If his father was white and his mother black, would he be called white? Or is it that the genes for blackness are dominant? If so, if a person is 1% black and 99% white, is he black? If not, what percent of black genes makes a person black? Or is it merely skin color? If so is an albino person, whose parents were both 100% Negroid, a white person? Is a Caucasian lifeguard with a dark tan black? Or is it the heaviness of the supra-orbital ridge, the size of the nose or jaw, or the basketball playing ability?

But it's more than just the words we use. A great part of our communication is non-verbal. For example, Iranian speech is not like American speech, Iranians are more likely to tell you what you want to hear rather than what they actually mean. Symbolism and vagueness are the rule, rather than the exception. So, the meaning of a word or a phrase spoken by an Iranian, while it might be understood by another Iranian, will probably be misinterpreted by an American or an Englishman. The real meaning can be hidden.

So, when we try to understand someone, there are not only the various meanings of a word, there is also the meaning given to it by the speaker or the writer. So how do we label our meanings so that others can clearly understand what we intend to be understood. Should a fly without wings be called a 'walk'? Is there another word for synonym? What about the meaning of democracy, justice, socialism, God?

A political liberal is probably for equality, socialism, and maybe communism. But a liberal education is supposed to make one freer in thinking and may develop conservative tendencies—because here 'liberal' means liberty or freedom.

Americans in Iraq called the people who were fighting them 'terrorists.' People in Iraq who were against the American invaders called them resistance fighters. What is the difference between freedom fighting and terrorism? Is there an overlap? What is a terrorist?

On the Ides of March were Brutus and his crew terrorists, freedom fighters or jealous politicians. When people accused Socrates of corrupting the minds of the young which eventually caused his death, was the accusation terroristic? The inquisitors were certainly terrorists, did their supposedly good intentions excuse them? If so, are Palestinian terrorists excused? Were Jewish terrorists in the 1940s, both before and after being given part of Palestine, justified in their guerrilla warfare?

Weren't the Crusaders terrorists? Darius, Cyrus, Alexander, Genghis, and Attila—what about them? The Nazis? And, of course, today the main threat comes from a group of violent Moslems. Should they be called fundamentalists? Would Mohammed have sanctioned such killing of innocents? Not according to the Qur'an! They may want to call themselves fundamentalists, but if you call yourself an elephant, you'd better have big floppy ears and an extra long nose.

Wasn't it terrorism to feed the Christians, or even Daniel, to the lions. Was it terror to have gladiators fight to the death? Was it terror when the Vikings attacked England and Ireland? Was it terror when the Spaniards decimated the Aztecs or when the American army wiped out the native Americans. And what about the Japanese in China, the Chinese under Mao, the Communists under Stalin?

What about the word 'freedom'? Freedom can be viewed as independence or as being exempted from certain proscriptions. But philosophers and lawgivers have never intended it to be a license to behave in anti-social ways. Were you to ask Rousseau or Jefferson whether pornography should be allowed to children, whether adults should be able to have sex with children, whether automatic weapons should be allowed to every citizen, or whether gratuitous violence should be allowed in the media--we can assume that these lovers of freedom would draw a strong line exempting such behaviors from the practice of freedom.

Democracy means that all citizens of a certain age can vote. The democracy of classical Athens didn't allow most of its inhabitants to vote because most were women or slaves.

Modern leaders have quite different concepts of this much revered word. For some it is only the right to vote. For others it includes many rights and ideas that go far beyond the generic roots of the word. Does democracy mean: everyone votes, men only vote, freedom of speech, freedom of religion, freedom to do business, or a myriad of other ideas far from its original meaning.

When the Afghan man who had converted from Islam to Christianity was brought to trial, facing the death penalty for giving up Islam, many thought his predicament was undemocratic in a democracy. Afghanistan had become a democracy, elected its representatives, and decided that the Koran was the supreme law of the land. There should have been no problem with the Afghanis approach to law. Democracy only means that the people decide. There have been very few real democracies in the world. They only work in small populations, like Swiss cantons and New England town meetings.

The big democracies are really republics. Most have democratically elected leaders, although in the U.S.A. that is questionable. The Americans have a sort of double republic when it comes to electing their president. The people of each state vote for people to vote for them. The majority in the state gets all the electors. Then they go to the electoral college and all the electors from the state vote for, or should vote for, the candidate of their party. If the Americans didn't have this 'electoral college' idea, Al Gore would have been president-- he had more than a half million more popular votes than George Bush. The world might well have been a different place: if the Americans had used the popular vote as every other democracy does; if the Supreme Court, in 2000, had had more Democrats than Republicans; or, if Al Gore's brother had been the governor of Florida instead of George Bush's brother.

Other American elections are more straight forward. The whole state votes for its senators, but for the House of Representatives the districts can be skewed or gerrymandered so that some districts become 'safe' for one party.

So, 'democracy' today only means that the people vote. Republic means that the representatives make the decisions. The meaning of democracy does not include tolerance, such as tolerance for a religion or a race. 'Democracy' does not mean a welfare state and social responsibility. It does not mean capitalism. It does not mean free trade. It does not mean equality before the law. It does not mean freedom of speech or of the press. It does not mean equality of educational opportunity. These are often understood in the West to be part of the democratic way—but they need _not_ be a part of a democratically elected government.

When the West pushed for democracy in the Mideast, they expected that those democracies would follow the mold of the West. Westerners were chagrined and disappointed. Their efforts were rewarded with a democratically sanctioned theocracy—a government by God. They were now dealing with a democratically empowered government of fundamentalist mullahs. It was actually easier to deal with the pragmatic strong men who often ruled the countries than it was to deal with imams, democratically empowered warlords, and newcomers unaware of the benefits and problems that had become the handmaidens of Western democracies.

Justice means fairness. But what is fair? Should 4-year-olds be allowed to have freedom of speech? Should jailed felons be allowed to vote? Should the death penalty be allowed? Should adult minorities be subject to the prejudices of the majority? And how many people think that justice often requires revenge.

Materialism, as a metaphysical term, means that there is no God and everything in the universe is physical. But it has taken on another meaning in that it often means the pursuit of material wealth—of money and goods. When an individual is only directed by the pursuit of money, the values of loving and unselfishness are left behind. Yet how often are these considered to be the highest values for an 'enlightened' society.

Private enterprise means that people should be able to develop their own means of economic production for their own survival. Total state control as in communism, where the state owns all of the means of production, or socialism, where the state owns some of the means of production--are contradictory ideas to free enterprise. However, under the socialism espoused by Karl Marx the state could own all of the means of production but would pay people based on their individual levels of production. But under Marx in a communist society all people would be given what they needed independently of what they produced. This lack of a selfish motivation was a major factor in the downfall of those countries that tried the communist experiment.

Capitalism actually means the system in which people make money from their own money, their capital, from investments, rather than from their physical work. While this may happen with full time stock traders, it does not happen with business owners who are actively running their companies as managers.

Many people lump together the ideas of democracy, and various freedoms, such as freedom of speech, capitalism, justice, private enterprise. We then have a confused set of meanings, so often discussions relative to any of these ideas are a hodgepodge of speakers howling from different Platonic caves misunderstanding the shadows cast by the semantic illusions they assume to be reality.

It amuses and chagrins many to see how the anti-abortion spokesmen shift biological definitions in their attempt to emotionally charge their audiences. At the South Dakota abortion law signing, the Governor referred to fertilized ova and embryos, and of course fetuses, as children. Often abortion foes call fertilized ova 'babies.' Nobody wants to kill babies or children!

Is it also correct to call 10-year-old children embryos or fetuses? If so, was it immoral to cut the umbilical cord? Shouldn't we all keep our umbilical cords tied into our mother's uterus? Webster defines "embryo" as an organism from conception to about two months of development and "fetus" as from two months until birth. One does not become a 'baby' or a 'child' until it is born.

Pro life anti-abortion groups chose a great slogan. Who would not be 'pro-life'? The questions that they haven't answered are: What is 'a life' or 'a human life'? Is it just a fertilized ovum? Is it a person who can take care of himself or herself—such as being able to find food, cook it, breathe, stay warm? Is it being able to contribute more to one's society than it takes from it? Is all life valuable, both human and non-human, as the Jain religion holds? Is an amoeba as valuable as a fertilized ovum? Is a monkey more valuable than a brain-dead person? Is it as moral to keep a pet, perhaps spending hundreds of dollars per month on it, as it would be to use that same amount of money on starving or diseased humans?

We might go a step farther in looking at the scope of South Dakota's laws. The state's rape rate is 30% higher than the U.S. average and more than double that of New York. Should the life of girls and women also be protected? Where does a rape conception fit into South Dakota's legislative priorities? Or is being pro-life only concerned with conception and not with sexual violence?

 Is all life equally valuable? The ancient Spartans placed their babies on a hill to see which would survive. The survivors then became valuable. Are the lives of draftees into the army valuable? What if the soldier was forced to serve, by being drafted? What about people condemned to death?

Was the life of Einstein equal to that of Hitler? Is a person who is brain dead but whose body is being kept functioning through nutrients in tubes and other functions provided by machines equal to a ghetto child in an underfunded school? Where should the government's funding go? Governmental funds are not unlimited.

Here's another semantic shuffle. The term *undocumented workers* means illegal aliens. Does that mean that we should use the term 'undocumented pharmacists' for illicit drug makers and sellers? And I guess it would certainly include the Columbian and Mexican drug cartels. To be politically correct should we call white slave traders 'undocumented travel agents?' And 'undocumented economists' or 'undocumented bankers' could include money launderers, people involved in protection rackets or 'Cosa Nostra' members. Certainly, law breakers deserve a semantic serape to give them respectability.

Genocide is another emotionally charged word usually used when an ethnic, racial or religious group thinks its numbers will be or are being reduced. So all wars are genocidal.

The word *God* has many meanings. We all think we know what the speaker means when we hear it. But do we mean the personal God of many in the West, the pantheistic god of the Hindu, a vengeful god or a merciful god, the deistic god of Jefferson or the meaning that some scientists, like Einstein, use meaning 'the wonder of the universe and the laws of physics.' This use of the term 'god' by many scientists does not mean a creating law-giving being.

For many Americans the sins of the body, that St. Paul warned us about, and the practices of the Puritans and Quakers in early America have made it almost impossible to call urination, defecation or toilets by their correct names. And the joy of orgasm is trashed by the use of so many negative epithets to substitute for the action of a loving sexual intercourse.

So, the question is--do we make sense when we talk? Do we mean what we say? I remember a girl I saw at the beach. She got angry with her dog. She yelled 'God damn you.' Did she mean it? She obviously believed in a Supreme Being and a Hell. That puts her well within the Judeo-Christian tradition. She must also have believed that her dog had an immortal soul. That puts her well outside of the Judeo-Christian tradition. So, what she said was not rational for most Americans. Of course, it was merely an unthinking psychological reaction to her frustration.

When the car won't start do you say 'God damn it' hoping that God will put your car into hell forever, melting it into a puddle of iron? And if you call someone a bastard, are you certain that his parents were not married? What if you call someone a 'son of a bitch' it might be more correct to say 'you are a human with dog-like qualities' or perhaps 'your mother must have had bitch-like qualities and you have inherited them.'

Look at the all-purpose use of the 'F' word—as a noun, verb, adjective, or interjection. It almost never means what it originally meant in the Germanic or Anglo-Saxon languages. But it takes no imagination to use it and it makes us feel profane and powerful. Listen to the literal meaning next time you hear it. 'Fuck you' means that the utterer wants you to have an orgasm. My fuckin' car stalled indicates that your automobile has a lover that is taking its energy away from its primary job of transporting you. Every time you hear the 'F' word uttered or screamed just substitute 'sexual intercourse' for the term and you will understand the real meaning of the speaker.

So relative to our correct use of words, we either don't know the correct word to portray our meaning, we don't define our words, or we react psychologically and use terms meaninglessly—making ourselves look uneducated to those who are educated. If we are going to think comprehensively or communicate clearly, we must have a clear understanding of the terms we use. And if we are communicating our ideas, we must define our terms so that our audience understands what we mean.

What people mean by God or gods varies depending on their definition of a natural or supernatural power. It seems that historically religious thinking has moved from animism, ancestor or nature worship to pantheistic or monotheistic ideas, then as people become more educated about history and empirical science, belief shifts to deism or to agnosticism or atheism—which rely more on the hope of humankind's potential than in the whims of a non-proved supernatural.

Strange but some Christians think that when Muslims worship Allah they are worshiping a different God. But Allah is just the Arabic word for the same monotheistic God that the English-speaking Jews and Christians worship. In fact, Arabic speaking Jews and Christians use the word Allah, just as English speakers use the word God, French speakers use Dieu and Germans use Gott. The point is that if we are not clear in our meaning of a term we will be as confused as the people listening to us. And, of course, we have to understand the exact meaning of the term being discussed and not be fooled by some inexact or emotional use of the term.

We must be aware that some people employ words for the purpose of disguising their thoughts. Others use absurdities to try to make their points. Nigerian Anglican Bishop Akinola has said that a homosexual relationship is a partnering of baboons. People often talk about addictions, addiction to work, addiction to food and so forth, But the medical meaning of addiction is physical dependence. If you don't get what you are addicted to-- your body rebels. We all know about heroin or alcohol addiction. And some people's bodies seem to be addicted to exercise. But people are not addicted to gambling or to chocolate. The desire to partake of these things is called habituation or mental dependence.

Sadly, far too few people have thought through their beliefs and clarified their language so that they can think and communicate effectively. A lack of vocabulary seems to be so common today when so few people read good books and so many watch television programs geared to the fourth-grade level. I remember that a TV personality referred to somebody as niggardly. Some illiterate African-Americans reacted, thinking that it was a racial slur. Niggardly, as any fifth-grade student should know, means selfishly or miserly. I wonder if Native Americans reacted negatively when communists were called 'reds.'

In 2020 a USC professor in a graduate business communication class was teaching an online class and mentioned that when we are speaking and can't find a word immediately, we may say 'a,' "er," or just pause. In Mandarin Chinese instead of a pause the speaker might say 'nèi ge' (pronounced NAY-guh). Black students complained that it was a racial slur and negatively affected their mental health.

It reminds me of what Robert Gordon Sproul, the most distinguished of the presidents of the University of California, once said, 'The function of the university is to make students safe for ideas, not to make ideas safe for students."

So, the USC professor was placed on a temporary suspension. The information he was passing on might have been viewed as interesting. It might also be critical to know it. Since this was a master's level class in business, what if sometime in the future one of these Black students is negotiating with a Chinese businessman, who pauses because he cannot find the correct word in English, and in pausing he says 'nèi ge.' And, what if the Black negotiator thinks he has heard 'nigger' and blows up at the Chinese man—thereby blowing the business opportunity. Taking it a step farther—what if he is fired from his job. What the Chinese man intended and what the Black businessman understood were poles apart. A rather important semantic misunderstanding.

But it is not only Chinese words that have sounds that can be misinterpreted by English speakers. It should not surprise any educated person that various languages may have words that do not have the same meanings in English.

➢   If a Scandinavian business man tells an American business woman, who is late to an appointment, 'You are slut.' The American would be insulted. But 'slut' means 'late" in Norwegian, Swedish and Danish. But this would never happen because the average Scandinavian has a better command of the English language than most Americans, having studied English every year in school.

➢   If you are driving in Norway and see a sign 'Farts-kontroll' at the instant you are about to pass gas, you may squeeze your buns together. But 'fart' in Norwegian means 'speed.' The sign was a warning that the speed limit will soon be reduced or that radar boxes may record your speed, and if you are speeding you may soon expect a speeding ticket in the mail. It can also mean that "speed bumps" are ahead. And be forewarned, the speeding ticket will cost you about ten times what it would have cost you in the USA!

➢   But if you were in France and someone wants to give you a fart, it would be a pet.

➢   If you are an American businessman talking to a Russian businessman and the Russian says, 'You are a brat,' don't be upset. He just called you a brother.

➢   And don't tell a Swede that you would like to 'kiss her all over,' because kiss (kyssa) means urinate.

➢   If you remind your Norwegian girlfriend to flush her poop down the toilet, she may leave your sadistic relationship because "pup" (pronounced "poop") is her female breast.

➢   And if you say push (puxe) in Portuguese, it means pull.

➢   If you were having breakfast in France and asked for strawberry preservative on your bread, the waiter might wonder why you wanted a strawberry condom on your baguette!

➢   If you were to tell a Romanian that he is 'full of crap,' he might wonder why you think his full of fish!

➢   If you were to tell a German or Scandinavian that 'I would like you to take this gift,' they might wonder why you want them to take poison.

Heaven help those business students from USC when they leave Los Angeles for the wider world! Even if they only get as far as London, they should learn quickly that a fag is a cigarette, not a homosexual, and a lorry is a truck, not a nickname for Laurence or Lorraine. But they should be comfortable when using 'taxi' or 'phone' since they are closer to universal in their meanings.

Trying to understand or discuss ideas is fraught with so many obstacles! The lack of an effective vocabulary. A lack of a common understanding of the terms we are using. An attempt to influence us by using inexact words or meaningless idioms. Whether it is the work of politicians or other charlatans, or merely the rationalizations of the unthinking—we must be vigilant that the truth is not twisted and stretched so that our minds are manipulated by semantic Svengalis.

Fake news and fake history have become major value and behavior manipulators. They have already had immense influence on American and British elections, and on our health with: anti-vaxxers, and the freedom-shouting people during the COVID pandemic who refused to wear masks, keep social distancing, or limit their meetings to very small groups. Such exhibitions of individual liberty were directly responsible for the large number of cases and deaths in the U.S., the UK, Brazil, and Sweden. In every country, when the known preventatives were relaxed, the cases surged.

If we can actually think our way along the path of truth, we must not be sidetracked by amorphous meanings or erroneous evidence. The silver-tongued possessors of ultimate knowledge, and the unbounded confidence of those who seek to influence us, are the ever-present nemeses of cool logical thinking. We can't intelligently discuss values without a clear idea of the concepts we are discussing.

INDUCTIVE LOGIC

A second area of logic is called inductive logic. Here we look at how probable is the truth of your statement. An opinion does not make it true, but of course your opinion may be true. If you say "all Mexicans are illegal immigrants." This is of course false because there are millions of people from Mexico who are American citizens. Some may be only American citizens, others may hold dual citizenship. And, remember that the southwestern states of the USA, from Texas to California, were owned by Mexico prior to the 1840s. The US went to war to aggressively gain a great deal of Mexican territory. I'll bet the Mexicans wish they had built a wall from northern California across to Colorado and down to Texas before the war. Even if they had paid for it themselves, they would be way ahead financially!

So, we are looking at the argument, and not who said it. Very often we assume something is true because of who said it: the Pope, the king, the candidate. What is the probability that United Kingdom will be better off after leaving the EU? What was the probability that invading Iraq and getting rid of Saddam Hussein would give birth to ISIS? What was the probability that Donald Trump could make America safer?

There are always people who are not happy with all that the government is doing. They may want: better primary education, better roads, free college tuition, a war with Iran, higher taxes on the rich, lower taxes, higher wages, better and cheaper healthcare, a balanced budget, a reduction in the national debt, and a number of other wishes. No government can make everyone happy, so in every election cycle there is the opportunity for the "out" politicians to promise the moon. When the "ins" haven't delivered it, we vote back in the rascals we voted out in the last election.

It is standard political procedure to play on the anger and disappointment of the population and promise them hope, if they will vote for you. In the West, in recent times, we have had some semblance of irrationality in the political discourse. In the last several years we have had George W. Bush, Brexit, Boris Johnson and Donald J. Trump strike down rational thinking and promise us things that sound good but are highly detrimental to our nations.

TALK ABOUT UNINFORMED VOTERS

➤40 percent of Trump voters insisted that he won the national popular vote.

➤60 percent of Trump voters thought that Hillary Clinton received millions of illegal votes.

➤73 percent of Trump voters believed that George Soros was paying anti-Trump protesters.

➤29 percent of Trump voters don't think that California votes should be allowed to count in the national popular vote.

➤67 percent of Trump voters thought that the unemployment rate went up under President Barack Obama. Only 20 percent accurately believed it went down.

➤39 percent of Trump voters thought the stock market went down under Obama. And 19 percent were unsure.

➤14 percent of Trump voters thought that Hillary Clinton was connected to a child sex ring run out of a Washington pizzeria. Another 32 percent weren't sure one way or another. Only 54 percent are certain that "Pizzagate" was a myth.

Millions of people vote straight party lines or they vote on information that is not correct. Those who believed Trump were believing statements that were found to be 50% totally false, 20% mostly false, and less than 20% of what he said was true or partially true. There was plenty of publicity on the truth and falsity of the statements by both presidential candidates, but the Rust Belt voters either didn't know or didn't care. What does this say about intelligently voting in our democracy?

People who want to lead a nation or to vote intelligently for representatives need much more information today than ever before. We need an extensive knowledge of world history, macroeconomics, natural science, biological science, the theory of science, philosophy of religion, comparative religions, political science along with some knowledge of psychology and sociology and an understanding of ethics. Armed with a strong background in basic knowledge we can then effectively criticize or agree with propositions that are held by candidates who want to run our governments. We should remember that empirical science is true—whether or not it jibes with your opinions. And, your opinions may not be true—no matter who told you to believe them.

Donald Trump was an anti-intellectual politician. He changed his position on major issues from week to week, possibly depending on the audience he was addressing. Changing a position is not wrong if you have additional evidence to make you change your mind. Ethically it is wrong if you're only changing it for political motives and do not plan to follow through with policies that implement your position.

About a month after taking office Trump cited a Muslim terror incident in Sweden two days prior. The fact was that there never was such an incident, it was a fabrication. When asked about it he said that someone had told him. He did not name the someone. Conversely, less than a week later an article appeared in the New York Times from an unknown source that criticized him. He insisted on the source being named. This waffling back and forth based on his actions and words and how they were reported and negatively impacted on him. It created not only concerns but also a number of questions about his psychological health.

In inductive logic we are looking at the probabilities of a statement. In the classic syllogism:

All men are mortal.

Socrates was a man.

Therefore, Socrates was mortal.

While it is true, as far as we know, that all humans born more than 150 years ago are dead. With work being done on artificial organs and blood, cloning and stem cell research—perhaps some humans in the future may be immortal. The second term 'Socrates was a man' may be open to question, but there is a great deal of historical evidence for him from contemporaries such as philosophers Plato and Xenophon and playwrights, such as Aristophanes. There are many references from others. So, we can assume that he existed. But what if we say that:

Democracy is the best form of government.

The U.S. is a democracy.

So, the U.S. has the best form of government.

As we have discussed earlier, democracy has many meanings, from: direct democracy, to a democratic republic, to a capitalistic economic system, to a welfare state—and many more meanings. So, we had better understand the exact semantic meaning of the speaker before we can proceed. So, as it stands, the argument is impossible to understand. There are many possible chinks in what we think is our armor of argument. These we call fallacies.

There are a large number of fallacies that relate to inductive logic. Often, they are not used to deceive, but the arguer has opinions that do not stand up to scrutiny. When Tea Party advocates were "definitely" against socialism, but could not define what it was that they were against? It was just ignorance-- not malice.

INDUCTIVE FALLACIES SEEN IN VALUES IN RECENT ELECTIONS

Because a number of inductive fallacies have been used extensively lately, we will give you an abbreviated list to give you an idea of how so many magicians of the mouth have attempted to pull the wool over our brains in their quests for political power.

When listening to candidates who are attempting to become elected today, we often hear statements that are not true, fake news, and promises that are impossible to fulfill. Many of these can be analyzed in terms of their truth or falsity. Many of these are what we call "logical fallacies." Here are just a few illustrations.

One common type of fallacy is called an **argumentum ad hominem**. (The argument is false because of the person who said it.)

Donald Trump criticized former Florida governor Jeb Bush in this way several times in their primary debates in 2016. He said that Bush: "had no honor," "was a hypocrite," "has no clue," and a number of other epithets that had nothing to do with the arguments that Bush was making. At various times, he called him: sad, desperate, a total disaster, a low energy guy, a sad sack, a low energy stiff and in many other negatives without criticizing his arguments. Bush was a major candidate with good credentials but was embarrassed out of the primary race.

Among the positions that Jeb Bush had taken were:

➢No litmus test for judicial appointees,

➢Abortion OK if the life of the mother was at risk,

➢Defund Planned Parenthood,

➢Aim for 4% national economic growth,

➢Bank bailouts were necessary,

➢For a balanced-budget,

➢Let businesses express religious freedom against homosexuals,

➢Lower tax rates on businesses,

➢For school vouchers,

➢A skeptic on global warming.

These conservative-reactionary positions actually agreed with Trump on many of the conservative-reactionary Republican positions. If an intelligent debate were going to be accomplished, they needed to argue about those areas in which they disagreed. Instead Bush was personally attacked, but his issues were not discussed.

Trump called US Senator Marco Rubio "a lightweight" 19 times that I counted.

On John Kasich, the Governor of Ohio, Trump called him: a typical politician, poor, doesn't have what it takes, can't debate, dummy, one of the worst presidential candidates in history, a total failure, so easy to beat, total dud, pathetic.

Then in his presidential run, he convinced many that there were secret things in Hilary Clinton's emails. This was probably the major factor in his winning because he turned many people against her, doubting her honesty. Her ratings as a Senator and Secretary of State at times nearly reached 70%, but with successful TV entertainer and often successful businessman, Don Trump, continually assailing her honesty because of her private email server, her approval rating dropped into the 30s. When the FBI finally completed its analysis of her emails, nothing was found that would incriminate her.

In his presidency, Trump continued to blame Bush and Obama for whatever had gone wrong, such as the pandemic that started three years after Obama's term had ended. And since the President said it—it must be true.

Trump's major approach to winning the primaries and the general election was in criticizing his opponents, usually without any proof. While this is not sound, as an inductive argument, it works because so many people are primarily moved by their unconscious minds and their inferiority complexes. It makes us feel good when somebody else is put down. And research often shows that when you hear something about 20 times—you generally accept it as true.

Another type of logical fallacy is the "**argument from ignorance**." In this line of thinking a person claims that something is true because it cannot be disproven. This is an argument often used in religion to prove God. Trump said he could increase the Gross Domestic Product by 3% and maybe as high as 6%. He said he could eliminate the national debt in eight years. And in 3 ½ years he increased the national debt by $5 trillion, then by $7 trillion by the time he left office.

Brexit voters were told that their economy would improve. Their 2017 GDP rise was 1.5%, lowest of all EU countries—which averaged a 2.7% gain for the year. In 2018 it was 1.3% and in 2019, 1.5%. What happened to the unrealistic unprovable promises that the voters had been led to believe? Oh well, ignorance!

Another type of fallacy is called "**the appeal to the stone**." Here someone else's argument is dismissed because I say so, without any proof. I counted 27 times that Trump called Ted Cruz a liar. He also called him a number of other negatives like: hypocrite, not nice, cheater, nasty, desperate, and a big problem.

Ted Cruz had many of the same views as Trump. He was a free-trade advocate, against abortion, for gun rights, against the Affordable Care Act, hard line on immigration, denied climate change, and saw Iran as an enemy.

He did vary from Trump in advocating a flat tax and abolishing the IRS, and being against a higher minimum wage, Cruz also proposed eliminating the departments of: Energy, Education, Commerce and Housing and Urban Development. Should these issues have been discussed, or was it enough to forget them? Here we have a combination of dismissing the arguments because of who said them (ad hominem fallacy) and because Trump said so.

Sometimes fallacies are implied. For example, what is called the **anecdotal fallacy** deals with a personal experience that is supposed to counter the available evidence. Since Donald Trump said he was worth over $3 billion he must've been successful. That success in business would obviously carryover to success in government. Of course, there is no evidence of this would happen--only conjecture. (Actually, businessmen who have become presidents have been among our least effective presidents. We'll come to that in a few moments.)

Apparently, no one in history disregarded provable facts anywhere near as much as Donald Trump, his statements will be used extensively to indicate some of the fallacies that run counter to verifiable scientific or historical facts.

"My child is autistic because she was vaccinated. I've heard of others on Facebook who have had the same experience." Of course, most children are vaccinated against a number of serious, and often fatal, diseases, There is no proof that any vaccinations cause autism. But there is proof that drug use, particularly cocaine, by the mother during pregnancy significantly increase the chance of autism.

And there is increasing evidence that marijuana use by the father, before conception, may also be linked to autism. The mother's use of cannabis is also related to autism. While the causes seem to be genetic and epigenetic, and are active primarily in the first two months of the pregnancy, months or years before any vaccination was administered, people look for excuses that make them blameless for the condition of their children. But the truth is that it was in their genes, for which they cannot be blamed, or in early epigenetic changes, for which they might be responsible.

The anti-vaxxers would be well advised to look at science, rather than social media, for their information.

There is also the "**appeal the probability**" fallacy. Here the arguer postulates that this would probably be the case. In the Brexit campaign, it was held that a return to sovereignty by leaving the EU would bring all sorts of positive effects. Trump's slogan "to make America great again," somehow assumed that the United States was not great even though it was the world's greatest economic power and it had the world's greatest military force. Trump gave no reasons why the country was not great, although we can assume that it meant that we needed more coal mining and steelmaking jobs.

The" **conjunction fallacy**" assumes that if one outcome is probable, so are many others. Trump made his case for "making America great again," this one slogan was supposed to carry over into creating jobs for coal miners and steelworkers, cutting down the murder rates in Chicago, moving illegal immigrants back to their home countries, cutting taxes for the rich, and marginalizing Muslims.

He then pushed the idea that illegal Mexicans were taking American jobs. But many of the jobs they did were "below the status" of Americans, like working in meat-packing plants and doing stoop labor in the agriculture field.

When the pandemic hit, Trump told America that is was just another version of the flu; that it would disappear when the weather warmed; and, that they were doing better than any country in testing. But the testing was ineffective, as was the tracing.

Then there is the type of fallacy that tries to link a possible positive outcome to a previous but unrelated positive outcome. It can also be used to link a negative outcome to a possible negative outcome. For example, claiming that Hillary Clinton was responsible for the killing of an ambassador in Benghazi, it would therefore make her unreliable as a president. Of course, she was not responsible for the killing of her friend. But truth is not a requirement for propaganda.

Clinton could have brought up the more than a thousand cases in which Trump was a defendant in courts. Some of these were cases involving federal laws which he had violated. Some were cases in which he did not pay his contractors.

When Hillary was asked why she didn't attack him the way he attacked her she said that, Michelle Obama had told her that "when they go low we go high." She assumed that a higher level of ethical behavior would win when contrasted with his baseless fallacies. She was wrong. Most people say they want ethics in government, but the truth is that for many, their most basic needs and their need to fulfill their power drives is primary when it comes to voting. In the future politicians should say, "when they go low, we will go lower."

There is another type of "ad hominem" argument which is called "**poisoning the well**." If Hillary had done anything wrong in the past, she would do everything wrong in the future. This is without proving that anything was wrong with her emails or the Benghazi situation. Trump continued to bring these up as if they were major concerns for a future president. Another type of this argument is to abuse the arguer rather than answer the argument. This has been a major approach of Donald Trump.

Another common fallacy is called **incredulity** that is a lack of belief. If I don't believe something, it can't be true.

Trump did not believe that the Obama care health program was any good. Of course, he did not understand that what Obama wanted and what he got from Congress were two very different programs. When Trump worked to get a healthcare program through the House of Representatives, he said, "who knew that healthcare could be so complicated!" Then there is the disbelief in climate change by the deniers. They may cite sun spots or the normal variation of weather experiences to back up their position that human caused warming is not a problem. But the fact is that for more than 50 years the weather has warmed, that long a period is called "climate."

Still another fallacy is called the **argument from silence**. Here my argument must be true because there is no evidence against it. I am a good businessman therefore I will be a good president. There is no evidence against this since I am not aware of any. Actually, the evidence is that in the US in the last hundred years, businessmen have been among our worst presidents. The latest ratings are: Trump, the worst; Harding, 6th worst; Hoover, 9th worst; GW Bush 15th worst.

Another fallacy is called **equivocation**. Here a word with more than one meaning is used to confuse the issue. For example, when creationists say that "evolution is only a theory" they are confusing a common use of the word with the scientific use of the word "theory"-- which means an established highly probable idea based on extensive research. Einstein's theories of relativity are examples. The creationists are using a different definition of theory which really means just guessing. "I have a theory that if I bet on black on the roulette wheel five times I will win at least twice."

"Let's make America great again." What does "great" actually mean in Trump's pronouncements? Does it mean to go to war with Mexico again, like we did in the 1840s, and take more of their land so that we can be a larger country? Does it mean going back to the past when religions were stronger and abortion was not possible? Does that mean going back to the 1950s and 1970s when laborers' earnings were a relatively large percentage of the CEO's earnings?

"**False attribution**" is the use by an arguer of unqualified or fabricated statements to back up his position. Trump did this when he cited a Muslim flare-up in Sweden to prove his anti-Muslim ideas. The problem was that there had been no Muslim flare-up in Sweden. George W. Bush did this with his false accounts of John Kerry's lack of heroism in Vietnam. The Brexiteers did it when they asserted that the EU workers were using the healthcare system more than the British, so were tapping unjustly into the coffers of the UK. The truth was that European workers did not use the health service as much as the British did. They were also told that they could have the same deal with the EU that Norway had. But Norway's deal cost almost as much as the UK paid and Norway was required to take in EU workers and migrants—the same conditions the Brexiteers wanted to eliminate.

"A **false dilemma**" is presented when only two possibilities are given for a solution when there may be many possibilities. For example, saying that there are only two ways to deal with Islamic terrorism. Let them all in or keep them all out. In reality, there was already a very strong vetting process in place by the US government.

The fallacy of "**a single cause**" is another oversimplification of the facts in a very complicated world. Illegal Mexican immigration has brought in both hard-working contributing people and a criminal element. They did come illegally so can be returned, but what if they are contributing to the society? Is it the best option for America? A few years ago, in Norway an Indian family was sent back to India because they were no longer in danger. The parents had responsible jobs, the daughter was in medical school and the son had the highest grades in his high school. Did Norway hurt itself in this action?

An "**incomplete comparison**" is a fallacy in which not enough information is given to make an accurate comparison. Trump continually said that he had "inherited a mess" but the truth was that when he took over: the unemployment level was under 5%, the lowest since the 70s, the stock market had gone up for seven years, most of the soldiers had been brought back from the Mideast, and President Obama was respected around the world as a peacemaker. Trump brought up no evidence for his claim.

The "**red herring**" fallacy occurs when the arguer does not answer the question but brings up another, often unrelated, situation and emphasizes that. Trump and his advisers did this continually. The press brought up the possible collusion with Russia in the election, and Trump answers that there were millions of illegal voters, or he answers that he supports Article 5 in the NATO agreement.

Still another type of fallacy is based on the idea that because it has been repeated so many times it must be true--**argument by repetition**. "Hillary is crooked." Trump said this 192 times that I counted. This was in addition to calling her a liar, corrupt, a fraud and incompetent. His basis for this seemed to be primarily her emails on a private server and the fact that she had made a great deal of money speaking-- often to Wall Street firms. The fact that he had made more money borrowing from Wall Street firms did not seem to be an issue, at least to him. But, of course, in politics as he saw it, there are no rules except to win.

This is a major problem in the process of electing representatives in many democratic republics. Repeat the lies about the faults or your opposition or your own accomplishments, usually with a controlled press, and your chances of winning are increased. Zimbabwe with Robert Mugabe, South Africa with Jacob Zuma, and Putin in Russia are just a few of the elected dictators around recently. It is almost unbelievable that two are now gone because of the people's strong opposition to them. Venezuela's poor voted for a spreading of the wealth in 1998, but much of the educated part of the country left and the mismanagement of President Maduro left the citizens starving and ill.

The solutions to major problems are not as simple as politicians, or our limited knowledge, lead us to believe. In the 2500 years of democracies, some people have gained power by honestly proposing ideas that should improve the society. But there have certainly been large numbers of presidents and representatives who had lied to gain power and often maintain their power through the strong arms of the police and army. The ideal of "government of the people, by the people and for the people" is too often "government of the powerful, by the powerful and for the powerful." And gaining that power is not always done ethically!

There can be overlaps in these fallacies in that something that is said violates more than one fallacy type.

"I believe in God, everybody does and nobody can disprove it." While God may well exist, the fact that the idea cannot be disproven or that everyone believes it, does not prove it.

VARIABLES

An early study in New York City, about two months after the first cases of the COVID-19 virus were reported, found that the death rates among Black/African American persons was 92.3 deaths per 100,000 population and Hispanic/Latino persons (74.3 per 100,000). These were substantially higher than that of whites (45.2) or Asians (34.5). Why? Was there a genetic weakness to the virus in the Blacks and a strength in the Asians? Was the cause in the type of occupations that the dead had pursued? Was it that one group was more social—so had been exposed to more potential carriers of the virus? Were: drug usage, nutrition, age, physical fitness, lack of health insurance or some epigenetic factors responsible—and to what degree? Any, or all, of these variables might be somewhat responsible. (Race is only one variable.) In San Francisco a week later the new corona cases showed that 13.7% of cases were Asian, but they accounted for 52% of the deaths! 6.7% of Asians who contracted the disease died, 2.4% of Whites had died, 4.5% of Blacks, and only 0.5% for Hispanics. There must be other explanations!

But many people jumped on the race issue—how many Blacks were dying. Was it because more Blacks were in necessary occupations, like transportation, nursing, or police?

The more variables in a situation, the less probable is the conclusion.

CONFLICTS IN VALUES

In Sir Walter Scott's 'Ivanhoe', the fool Wamba ridiculed religious prejudice by arguing, 'For every Jew you show me who's not a Christian, Sir Knight, I'll show you a Christian who's not a Christian.' People often spout their versions of religious scripture to validate their behavior. But their behavior might be quite different from the message they should derive from their scriptures. In fact, what we deem as 'moral' behavior is not as clear cut as we would like to assume. Our own value decisions quite often jump around from being God-based to self-centered, to society-based. Few people are consistent, using one basic assumption for all of their value decisions.

Let's look at several ethical problems and see how you might be for or against each problem whether you take a self-centered, a God-based or a society-based assumption. In other words, finding the answers to moral questions is not as simple as many seem to think. While we may start with a self-, God-, or society-based assumption we will then add evidence to make our opinion clearer and stronger. And as we mentioned earlier, that evidence can be empirically verifiable or historical, it may have been given us by some authority, or it may just be our opinion.

As an example, let's assume that my opinion relating to mercy killing is based on my belief in God and the truth of the Bible. Perhaps I'm not as familiar with the Bible as I might be, but my minister has preached that mercy killing is wrong. But now my evidence changes because my mother is incurably ill and in terrible pain, she has asked me to help her die. I love my mother. It seems that the merciful thing to do is to help her to die. Do I abandon my God-based assumption and become self-centered because I want my mother to rest in peace? Do I search the Bible for new evidence that would show me that mercy killing is not against the Scriptures that have been basic to my life? Maybe there is other self-centered evidence. My mother has now used up the five million-dollar maximum on her health insurance. If I mortgage my house, I can buy another month of hospital care, but I had planned to re-finance my house to pay for my children's college educations. And remember, my mother wants me to help her die. She would definitely disapprove of my taking her grandchildren's legacy to pay for more life that she doesn't want. Do I 'accidentally' remove her breathing tube? Do I allow an air bubble to enter her bloodstream through one of her intravenous tubes? Do I simply give a 'do not resuscitate' order? Do I ask a doctor to give her more than the normal dose of morphine? Do I leave her to the hospital's care, letting it absorb the costs? But what if the hospital me you for the money?

Here we have self-centered feelings versus what we believe to be a God-based conflict. But often societal values are also important. Most of the greatest conflicts are between the self-centered values that I want right now and the other values, such as self-centered future values, or God or society values.

A survey of American physicians indicated that the majority felt that it is ethically permissible to explain their moral objections to patients regarding contraception, abortion and euthanasia. Over 80% said that they felt they should explain all of the options to the patient, but 30% would not refer a patient to another physician who did not share his or her moral beliefs. Being male or religious was more likely to reduce the chances of the patient being told all the options or of being referred to a doctor who shared the patient's point of view. (Curlin et al. "Religion, Conscience, and Controversial Clinical Practices," New England J. of Medicine. Vol. 356, No. 6, Feb. 8, 2007, pp 593-600)

People who use God-based assumptions believe that they are infinitely superior to self-centered and society-based values. The problem is that religious values are not universally held. Buddhist values differ from Jewish values, Christian values of one Christian vary from that of another equally devout Christian, Muslims differ among themselves. And, of course, the values of some atheists will be identical to values held by some religious believers. If all Christians believed the same, or if all Muslims believed the same, we might be able to formulate a code of ethics for that group of believers. But while most will agree on not murdering, just look at Muslims in Iraq killing other Muslims with bombs; look at Israeli Jews killing Palestinian non-combatives or Lebanese non-combative women and children. Or look at the good Christians who shoot Christian doctors who provide legal abortions, or good Christian Ku Klux Klansmen who burn down Christian churches and kill Christians of a different color.

A few years ago, a fatwa was issued against a female tennis player who was a Muslim because she wore short skirts, but no fatwa was issued against al Zarwari's killing of Shi'ite children or adults in the suicide bombing missions he ordered in Iraq. Should someone of authority prioritize religious values for every sect?

People who believe strongly in their ideas of God-based values will not accept the societal assumptions that the society must be based on a constitution and on a government of laws, because their concepts are superior to society's ideas of laws.

In 2011, Norway had a huge eruption of sentiment for a young woman, Maria Amelie, who had come to Norway with her parents illegally from Russia when she was 12. Without a state issued national identity number she went through Norwegian schools, graduated from college, then got her Master's degree. She then wrote a book about her experiences and won a Norwegian literary prize. When she was then discovered, she was forced to leave the country under Norwegian law. The publicity engendered, prompted a Norwegian company to offer her a job. But she had to leave the country first. Under the Napoleonic laws of Norway there was no other way. If she had been in a common law country like the US or the UK the judges could have found a loophole to keep her as being valuable to the society, but not under Napoleonic law, that seldom allows loopholes. For the good of society valuable people should be kept, but also for the good of society the laws must be upheld. So we had a conflict between her self-centered interests and society's interests, but we also had conflicts in the various interests of the Norwegian society.

SECTION IV   DO WE WANT IDENTITIES SELECTED INTELLIGENTLY?

Traditionally we:

➤ Wait for the problem rather than trying to prevent it. Tradition stands in our way!

➤ Evaluate the whole of a situation by what we observed at the end. Our shallow concern stands in our way!

➤ Blame others, when we had the option to avoid or change the situation. Our self-centered blinders stand in our way!

➤ Base our opinions on our emotions rather than our intellects. Our intellectual laziness stands in our way!

Recently many often believe:

➤ Most things we hear, read, or are told.

➤ Social media posts, no matter how uninformed the authors are.

CHAPTER 7 IF YOU DON'T KNOW EVERYTHING-- YOU DON'T KNOW ANYTHING

Look at the last few minutes of a situation--and you know the whole story. Very true, if you are a simpleton!

Liz Cheney was ousted from the third most important position in the House Republican Party in May of 2021. She was replaced by Elise Stefanik. Cheney voted with Trump 93% of the time, while Stefanik voted with him 78% of the time, according to one conservative evaluation group, while the American Conservative Union had Liz at a 78% rating and Elise at 44%. But the question is "What have you done lately?" Liz voted to impeach Trump for his role in the January 6th invasion of the Capitol. Elise didn't. Liz voted to affirm the clear election of Joe Biden. Elise didn't. Elise backed Trump's lie that the election was stolen from him--even though in Trump's 60+ court actions to overturn the election, he could not offer any evidence to support his case--even in courts where he had appointed the judge. Trump loyalists accepted his word without any evidence. But most in Trump's party accept his word over the evidence.

We see the last 9 minutes of George Floyd's life and his death, and he becomes an international icon. He was passing a counterfeit bill and was under the influence of a drug that was illegal under federal and state laws. There is no question that the penalty did not fit the crime for George. BUT, the area was a high crime area. CBS News ranked Minneapolis the 19th most dangerous city in the U.S., right behind Chicago. In 2017, the city had four times more rapes and robberies than the national average. And that doesn't even count the murders. The Powderhorn Park area of the city, where George Floyd was killed, had 18% more crimes than the rest of Minneapolis and 750% higher than the Minnesota average. In 2021 its homicide rate doubled over 2020. Was George Floyd more important to the world than the other 46 murder victims in Minneapolis? Was it only because his ordeal was filmed on a smart phone?

Is it the same degree of murder when you kill someone resisting arrest in Minneapolis as it is to kill the president of Haiti or the Grammy-nominated rapper and community contributor Nipsy Hustle. What about Robert Kennedy or Abraham Lincoln? Are all of our lives of equal worth?

Here are the recent statistics from the FBI for Minneapolis and Minnesota.

Statistic	Powderhorn Park /100k people	Minneapolis /100k people	Minnesota /100k people	National /100k people
Total crime	5,946 (estimate)	5,443	2,315	2,489
Murder	n/a	10.7	2.1	5.0
Rape	n/a	106.5	43.4	42.6
Robbery	n/a	299.1	55.8	81.6
Assault	n/a	509.5	135.1	250.2
Violent crime	1,300 (estimate)	926	236	379
Burglary	n/a	788.1	282.4	340.5
Theft	n/a	3,056.0	1,597.5	1,549.5
Vehicle theft	n/a	672.8	198.9	219.9
Property crime	4,646 (estimate)	4,517	2,079	2,110

Crime data for this area is not available from the FBI. Data from local enforcement agencies is analyzed and algorithms are applied to estimate the number of crimes in the area.

The police are charged with reducing crime and arresting criminals. What should be done?

> ➢ Reduce police funding.
> ➢ Eliminate the police.
> ➢ Talk nice to the violent criminals.
> ➢ Police are generally taught to meet force with superior force--is this effective?

How would you handle the situation--and what evidence do you have that your method is superior to what is being done?

CHAPTER 8   VALUES OR ETHICS ARE NOT SET IN STONE-- ALTHOUGH MOSES AND THE POPE WOULD LIKE THEM TO BE

MORAL RELATIVISM AND APPLIED ETHICS

The morals that people actually use are relative—relative to time, place, and situation. But popes and prelates, mullahs and moral philosophers, would have us all hold the same values. But the power or pleasure drives in us may entice us to act differently from our stated beliefs. Look at the Catholic priests violating young boys. Evangelical and main-line Protestant ministers more likely violating the opposite sex. Then there was Jerry Falwell Jr., president of the ultra-conservative Liberty University, who was released after his involvement in a six-year sex scandal involving a former pool boy, Falwell's ultra-conservative religious wife, and himself.

The Pope wants everyone to hold the same values that he does, what he sees as God-based values. But popes have been known to have girlfriends—and children!

The lawmaker who is for a woman's free choice wants everyone to agree with her. She doesn't want people, like the Pope, disagreeing because if his different values.

Marijuana smokers want their self-centered values to be freed from society's marijuana criminalization laws, even though there is no positive societal benefit from marijuana use—except for some medical uses. But the major reason, by far, is their desire to get high and not go to jail. Then we have a societal reason, since people are going to use the federally illegal drug, the costs to society of legal expenses and imprisonment, are high.

Values are relative to the point of view of the person holding the value, whether he or she believes it comes from God, from what is best for the society, or what is best for one's self. Values are "relative" even within a religion. A Catholic priest, working with AIDS victims or among the poor who are pushed deeper into poverty with each child, may believe in contraception in opposition to his bishop or pope who are against it. In Christianity a sect that ordains female ministers and bishops is not in step with the Catholic laws of ordination. If you don't agree with my ideas on war, gay marriage, cohabitation or any number of things, our values are relative—relative to our points of view, you are immoral! If we all used the same basic assumptions and had access to the same evidence, our values might not be relative.

The conflicts in values within one's own society are complicated when the values of another society conflict with yours. Such questions as the importance of money, the necessity of working, the need for a loving relationship, or the sanctity of life, and freedom of speech and assembly, are just a few of the areas where national differences are significant.

There is probably no way our values will ever be identical for every member of our species. So we just have to adjust. Adjust or bust! The best we can hope for is some consensus. I think that the great majority are against robbery, rape and murder. So, it is easy to make laws against them. But we might not have as much consensus on the punishments for breaking those laws. Long prison terms or capital punishment are options, but are not as universally agreed on.

So the realities are that we have a large number of ethical practices within each group of basic assumptions and also a great deal of crossover of ethical beliefs and practices between the people who advocate the different basic assumptions. So while each of us will be quite certain of the essential nature of our own ethical beliefs, as circumstances change we quite often shift our beliefs, and often then shift our basic assumptions to sanctify our new opinion. Just look at the United States Catholics, the Pope says no abortions, but the rate of Catholics undergoing abortions is similar to that of non-Catholics.

People like to sound very moral, often God-based, but what they actually do shows their true ethical beliefs. It is so common that it is almost a rule that a person judges himself by what he says—not by what he does. We behave in selfish ways then rationalize our behaviors to cover up our weaknesses. We discuss with great concern the illegal drug problem, while we drink our cocktails. We condemn the poor quality of our schools while we vote down new school taxes. We criticize our politicians but we don't vote, because it would take fifteen more minutes from our busy day once or twice a year.

So if we want to develop our identity intellectually we should start by looking at our behavior. If we don't act in accordance with what we say we believe--WHY? Should I change my behavior to be in accord with what I say? Or, should I be honest?

The reverend, and I use the word in a detrimental sense, Ted Haggard, a strong opponent of gay marriage and pastor of a 14,000 member mega-church and president of the 30 million member National Association of Evangelicals, resigned after being accused of a three year sexual affair with a male prostitute and buying methamphetamines from him. Representative Mark Foley was co-chairman of the House Caucus on Missing and Exploited Children, he resigned after admitting to soliciting his young male assistants. Strongly religious Tom DeLay resigned his congressional seat amid charges of corruption. But these are just the tip of the iceberg. DeLay and Foley should have been acting from society-based values in their Congressional jobs, but they acted self-centered, while saying they were God based. Very confusing!

Not many months later a 52 year old minister, one of 42 ministers in a Texas megachurch with 26,000 members, was arrested for sexual improprieties with one he thought to be 13 year old girl. It was part of a police sting. His arrest occurred after he had driven 200 miles to meet her.

Of course, wide discrepancies between what one practices and what one preaches is not limited to Christians. A number of the Muslin 9-11 hijackers drank hard alcohol—forbidden in the Koran (Koran 2:219), watched pornographic films, and went to nude bars where they danced with the nudes—both forbidden in the Koran (24:33), or desired or used prostitutes—also forbidden (24:2). One even left a copy of his Koran at a bar. If they believed they were promised paradise in a few days, why did their self-centered desires win out over their supposedly professed beliefs in the Koran?

In older days the God of the Mid-East was responsible for everything—death, disease, war. But for many modern people, with the often-supposed death of God and the rise in democracy, the individual has become responsible. A person's smoking or a lack of exercise causes disease, as does his high fat intake. His ideas and work ethic are responsible for his success or failure in his economic life. People, not God, are responsible for famine and AIDS, for war and yes, even for peace.

Another case of society vs. self-centered values is found in the numerous cases of individuals or states suing tobacco companies. I don't remember doctors ever advocating smoking—even though many used to smoke. Athletic coaches have always warned their charges against smoking. Schools have advised against it, as have public health agencies. I doubt that any smoker in the U.S. has ever believed that smoking was healthful. And if that smoker can read the warning on the cigarette package, he well knows that it can be 'hazardous to his health.' But for his self-centered desires to have 'pleasure now' through a nicotine jolt-- he smokes. Then when he develops emphysema, lung cancer or heart disease he sues the cigarette company. Or if he dies, his heirs sue the company. Courts, representing society, often give huge financial awards to people for their stupidity of having smoked.

While society should certainly continue to warn its citizens of the possible problems due to developing a nicotine habit, perhaps it should recognize that smoking can be good for society as a whole. If the cigarette taxes are high enough to more than pay for the hospital expenses due to the habit, the earlier deaths of the smokers will reduce the amount of retirement benefits that the society will have to pay. In fact, this was one of the reasons that a tobacco company gave an eastern European country for allowing smoking in that country.

There is a major question as to how much individual freedom a society can allow its citizens and still keep a semblance of order. It seems to be a universal rule that societies do not allow their citizens to murder or rape those in their own societies. But once we leave the bounds of our countries, particularly during wartime, even those rules are often broken. And, in fact, many of our greatest heroes are those who have killed the most humans who wore their enemy's colors. And how does the society enforce its laws? One culture cuts off the hand of a thief at the wrist. Another merely slaps that wrist.

SELF VERSUS SOCIETY

There seems to be no universally acceptable solution. I can't have everything I want. I must give up some of my self-centered values to gain other self-centered values. If I want a friendlier ecological society, some of my fellow citizens must reduce their expectations for parenthood. Yet none of us want to be told how to run our lives. There is the continual battle between individual and collective rights—the values of the self, pitted against the values of the general social good.

This was clearly illustrated a number of times in the covid-19 pandemic. People who wanted freedom, wanted their businesses open, didn't want to wear masks or get vaccinated--died a lot! In 2021 92% of covid deaths in the US were to unvaccinated people. The value of liberty, of individual freedom, over the more societal value of equality, killed many. Pressures of many groups, like the hospitality industry, combined with needing the tax revenue from businesses being open and people employed, pushed governments to open. In July of 2021, the UK opened up--despite seeing 50,000 new cases and 100 deaths a day. Within two days it was 100,000 cases. So maybe they should have waited a day or two!

So the call for individual freedom and the need for taxes conflicted with the need to keep more people uninfected and alive. Two desirable goals in conflict. Does opening up increase the costs of hospitalization, kill off valuable productive citizens, kill off non-productive citizens, kill off more members of the freedom-loving political party, increase tax revenue? It is reducing the world's population, which is the major ecological concern--but a large number of the deaths are to older people, who are no longer reproducing.

Even if we could somehow meet a happy medium between the desires of the individual and the general good of the group, we will undoubtedly still have conflicts between our self-centered and social values and the desires we might have to practice our religion the way we wish. It is so common as to be a rule that the self-centered, the society-centered, and the God-centered values will continue to conflict and to not allow for a mutually arrived at consensus—or more important, an intelligent approach to our problems.

There are a few countries in which the religion is so strong that its religious values are also the values of the society. The holy scriptures dictate the laws of those societies. This certainly makes the value system clear to the inhabitants of that country. In a Moslem country that uses the Koran as its law, the thief can certainly lose his wayward hand. Both Allah and the king have joined their hands on that issue. Shari'a, using the law of God as the law of the land makes perfect sense if: there is a God, and that God did in fact hand down His law to humankind, then that it was passed down without error from God's human spokesperson without changes in interpretation, and that God intended that the law was to be immutable and eternal and not meant to apply only to those people to whom He gave the law at the time and place that the law was given. One problem is that so many mullahs and caliphs have interpreted the law differently.

But what about a country, like my own, which values freedom of religion? If the religion dictates that we should produce as many babies as possible but the society holds that more babies are not good for the society-- what happens? Well, our courts have often determined that the practicing of a religion may be harmful for the society and therefore illegal. This has happened when the rights of society, as viewed by the courts, have more validity than the self-centered rights of the person to refuse medical care for himself or his child, because of a religious belief.

There was also a major case that held that people in a religious sect which handled poisonous snakes and drank poison to prove their holiness were behaving against the best interests of the society. The members of the Holiness Sect were doing just what the Bible had indicated as a test of holiness. After his resurrection, Jesus appeared to his apostles and told them that the believers 'shall take up serpents, and if they drink any deadly thing, it shall in no wise hurt them; they shall lay hands on the sick, and they shall recover.' (Mark 16:18) However the Court held that the society must protect its own citizens from themselves—no matter what the source of their beliefs. The state Supreme Court ruled that the citizens have the right to believe anything they want in the religious area but that their rights to practice that belief are limited to society's rules. But courts have ruled both ways on this issue.

This is probably why we don't allow any religions to sacrifice beautiful maidens to the god of the volcano. This I believe is a wise decision. There were just not enough beautiful maidens in the country—and sacrificing them was such a waste! Maybe instead, we older citizens should be tossed into the boiling cauldron!!

So which values should we hold most dear? Most of us would like to have our own freedom unrestricted, but we can all see ways to limit the liberties of others. It's OK if I drink and drive—but not if you do it. It is fine for me to take a sick day off from work to play golf but if you do it, you're cheating. I can drive my car beyond the speed limit but you should not.

But what if each of my selfish whims were punished by death if I were caught? Might society benefit from having fewer drunk drivers, cheaters, and speeders? And is the death penalty so bad? None of us will live forever! On this planet not many of us will make much of a positive difference in the future of the world. If we plan to have a strong societal ethic, such as that of Denmark, we will need either a highly effective system of education and strong social pressure or a penal system that insures societally correct behavior.

Is it possible to develop a consensus among the populace? I think not. We will, for the extended foreseeable future, continue to have conflicts based on our immediate desires. Our inferiority complexes, and our lack of ethical and ecological understanding will continue to stop the progress that must be made. The uninformed individuals will continue to fall in line with the commanders of their kingdoms and the regents of their religions. In short, as the philosopher Spinoza said, "The masses of people will always be ruled by imagination and emotion, not by reason."

If our minds are allowed to be free, we will always have conflicts in values. Orwell's Big Brother could not control all of the people. The Soviet KGB could not control all of the people. The powerful Pope of Rome has not been able to convince all of his faithful to follow of all of his pronouncements. There will always be thinking people. And those thinking people will hold different basic assumptions. Those varying assumptions and the types of evidence we choose to use with them will generate quite different ethical and political systems. If only God would descend to us and set us straight—but we wouldn't believe Her.

VALUE QUESTIONS

Let's discuss a number of value questions. Our values make up a very large part of our identities. I think we can see how most value questions can be seen as moral or immoral depending on which basic assumptions we use and what evidence we use with that assumption.

Let us look at some social considerations and how we might take self-centered, God-based or society-based assumptions as the starting points for seeing how our moral ideas may develop. We will look at an existing problem, like abortion or animal rights or capital punishment. Then we will add evidence, such as historical or empirical, to the mix and we will see that just about any problem can be seen as ethical from a self, God or society point of view—depending on the evidence we choose to believe.

All of these problems are problems with which societies must wrestle. We will start with some general social problems, then explore some ethical problems about life and death, then some issues about reproduction. Then I want to look at some problems that center on sex or marriage. As I have said, the positions people may take on one of these issues depends not only on their basic assumptions but also on the evidence they choose.

But more. Some aspects of our assumptions may move out of the nebulous area of assumptions and move more toward probability. While we cannot prove or disprove a supreme being, we may be able to provide more proof for individual or societal behaviors. If a hundred years ago a person assumed that opium would not hurt him, he had no proof. Today we do. The assumption of the Divine Right of Kings and their right to absolute rule, has been sociologically disproved as an effective method of government. So, our previous beliefs and assumptions are sometimes proven to be in error as our knowledge increases.

The various sciences of psychology, economics, sociology and such can measure more effectively the realities and the effects of some programs. Does capital punishment reduce crime? Does contraception or abortion make most people's lives happier? Is torture an effective way of gaining information from terrorists? Will euthanasia save a society money?

What are the advantages and disadvantages of the welfare state? These can be measured!

We looked at some issues concerning the welfare state as a possible ideal. Let us now look at it as being an ethical approach or a non-ethical way of handling a society. While we looked at the ideal of 'cradle to grave' state responsibility, because it exists today, we can measure it. When Karl Marx proposed his idea of communism it could not be tested. It was purely in the camp of societal basic assumptions along with Plato's Republic and Augustine's City of God. But as the Soviet Union struggled through its brand of socialism it was clear that peoples' human selfishness would not make Marx's ideas of socialism or communism universally accceptable today. Maybe in the future, but not today.

The welfare state continues to be an ideal. But the economic realities of globalization and the demands of the people are stretching it and causing many to question it. Can states provide more and more in today's world? Must the benefits be pruned back? How high can people be taxed without rebelling. Will the high-level producers leave the country because they rebel at paying for other people's benefits?